"A must read. *Thanks from Iraq* will enlighten you about the war in Iraq and touch your heart."

Paul Skousen: Intelligence Analyst for the CIA and Regan White House, Author, Lecturer and Editor.

"This book laments the tragedy of war while at the same time acknowledging it is a justifiable necessity. It is a responsible commentary on our frustrating human condition."

COL James Kinney,
Senior COL at Madigan Army Medical Center.

KELLY FAUCETTE
#0206
Kelly J Faucette

To Robert E Poulson,

Thanks for your support.
I hope you enjoy this book.
May the Lord bless you.

Thanks from
IRAQ

COL KELLY J FAUCETTE M.D.

Thanks from
IRAQ

SHOULD WE BE THERE?

THOUGHTS, EXPERIENCES, AND
LETTERS OF THANKS WHILE DEPLOYED

TATE PUBLISHING & *Enterprises*

Published by Tate Publishing & Enterprises, LLC
127 E. Trade Center Terrace | Mustang, Oklahoma 73064 USA
1.888.361.9473 | www.tatepublishing.com

Tate Publishing is committed to excellence in the publishing industry. The company reflects the philosophy established by the founders, based on Psalm 68:11,
"The Lord gave the word and great was the company of those who published it."

Book design copyright © 2008 by Tate Publishing, LLC. All rights reserved.
Cover design by Isaiah R. McKee
Interior design by Nathan Harmony

Published in the United States of America
ISBN: 978-1-60604-315-8
1. Autobiographical-Current Events   2. War-Iraq
08.06.23

DEDICATION

This book is dedicated to my fellow soldiers who leave family and friends to deploy, and to all those who support the soldiers and send so much to help spread peace and good will. Families worry so much and their prayers are very much felt and appreciated. It is especially dedicated to my wife, Sharon. She had to take over so many things and performed flawlessly. It is dedicated to my four children and granddaughter who I love dearly.

The information and opinions in this are solely that of the author and do not represent those of the United States Army.

ACKNOWLEDGEMENT

I wish to thank several individuals who encouraged me to write after reading my first letter which I wrote late one night when faced with taking care of an insurgent who made bombs and a group of children who were severely injured by an explosion in a marketplace. These include doctors Alexander Niven, Gregory Lee, Thomas Curry, and Alec Eror who are also close friends and fellow soldiers. One of the chapters was written by another friend and colleague, Dr. Rochelle Wasserman. I wish to thank Paul Skousen, Tony Munoz and my fellow Madigan pediatricians, Donald McClellan and James Kinney who read the letters and encouraged me to publish them and David Estroff who did a proof reading.

TABLE OF CONTENTS

FOREWORD

All who know Dr. Kelly Faucette know him to be a man of true faith, a man who has dedicated his life to service; service to God and his church, service to his family and service to his fellow man. Dr. Faucette chose early in his medical career to commit his skills to one of the most emotionally demanding of all specialties, Pediatric Oncology, the care of children with cancer. In ministering to some of the most gravely ill children he would often be called upon to try and explain to loving parents, "why?" a question all physicians wrestle with at one time or another. These difficult discussions are usually held within the hallowed halls of an outstanding Army Medical Center. Rarely, if ever, were Army pediatricians called upon to serve in a war zone. After all, they signed up to care for the children of Military families! However, given his renowned expertise in the care of severely ill children, his true patriotism and his willingness to share the burdens of others, COL (Dr.) Kelly Faucette volunteered to serve in Iraq. As Chief of the Department of Pediatrics at Madigan Army Medical Center, Ft Lewis, Washington he did not have to do this. This action alone demonstrates clearly the type of man Kelly Faucette is. However, in doing so he placed himself in a world so different than any he had known before he now had to ask himself "why." Why do I save the life of a man who lives to kill me solely because I am an American? Why do children who know no politic and worship a loving deity have to suffer at the hands of extremists and why do American Soldiers remain so dedicated to the task that once healed they desire to return to their brothers in arms?

In the pages that follow you will read Dr. Faucette's daily thoughts as he answers the questions for himself and perhaps for you, the reader. As the man who emphatically informed him that he did not have to take this assignment, I am humbled everyday by his actions and ethic. I hold him in the highest esteem and I am sure after reading his story you will too.

COL (Dr.) George McClure
Deputy Commander for Clinical Operations
Western Regional Medical Command
Fort Lewis, Washington

INTRODUCTION

Each person who serves in Iraq has a unique experience. Each soldier has a story they could tell. Each life has value and their stories are worthwhile.

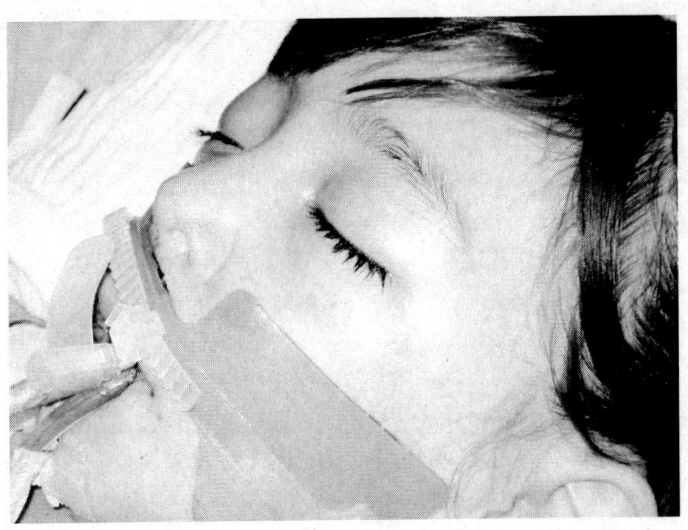

*A severely injured Iraqi girl, Iesha, sheds
a tear while on the ventilator*

Dear Reader,

Thank you for choosing to read this book which is a collection of letters and stories. I hope that you enjoy it and find it helpful. It contains some of the experiences and feelings that I had when I was deployed. When I was in Iraq a reporter came to our hospital and asked us "in a word" to describe our experiences there. My answer to that question would be "enlightening." I hope that this book is enlightening to you.

The title, *Thanks from Iraq*, was chosen because thankfulness is a summary of the final feeling in each letter. I realize that *Thanks from Iraq* might be a bit confusing because the book was not written from the Iraqi people, but in Iraq. I do feel that most of the Iraqi people do feel great thanks for what has happened there. I wanted to tell America of the things I learned. There were so many people to thank for the enlightening, life changing experiences which I had. I developed a great appreciation especially for the soldiers who put their lives on the line to help bring an end to tyranny and the threat of terrorism. I appreciate their courage and desire to make the world a better place. I especially appreciate their families and loved ones who worry about them each day. Some of them gave the ultimate sacrifice of their very lives. Their families also gave a near equal sacrifice in the loss of their son or daughter, husband or wife, or father or mother. I learned to appreciate the Iraqi people I got to know. These include the fathers of children who were in the hospital, soldiers, policemen and interpreters who put their lives on the line to stand on the side of freedom. I grew to know and appreciate the nurses, medics and doctors with whom I worked. We were in a relatively safe place, a forward operating base in Mosul and do not consider ourselves heroes, but did work with true heroes, the young soldiers who were out and about on the roads and in the cities, in harm's way every day. They did their jobs with honor and integrity. They made me proud and indeed thankful.

Each person who serves in Iraq has a unique experience. Each soldier has a story they could tell. Each life has value and their stories are worthwhile. During my time in Iraq I tried to talk to as many people as I could to find out their stories and how the war had affected them. I talked to as many Iraqis as I could and learned that they are good people. I learned that we are not fighting Iraq, but are fighting a common enemy who would take away freedom and to whom life has little value or meaning.

As I wrote these letters I shared some of them with my fellow physicians. One of them, Dr. Rochelle Wasserman, said that she had written a letter to her son, which I liked very much and found to be touching, insightful and poignant. I asked her if I could include it if I were ever to publish my letters and she gave me her permission to do so. That letter is entitled "The Missive" and is thus included with my letters. I thank her for letting me include it.

After a few weeks in Iraq I had an experience taking care of a little girl who had nearly been killed by a bomb, and then faced an insurgent who made bombs and felt within me feelings that I had never felt before. That evening, unable to sleep, I got out of bed and wrote of that which I was feeling, and thus began a weekly letter to my family and friends sharing some of the experiences and thoughts that I had. These letters are the substance of this book.

In the end, the one question I have often been asked is whether we should be in Iraq or not. I hope that as you read this book, you gain some additional insight which will help you answer that question in your own mind.

Thanks to you for reading it and if you enjoy it or find it helpful, perhaps you could pass it on, or put in a good word for it. Thank you.

COL Kelly J Faucette M.D.

THE DOCTOR'S DILEMMA:

A Draining Abscess
and an Insurgent

"All people have worth. I will try to forgive. I do not understand him, the man lying in the bed with the bandanna over his eyes; I don't think that I can."

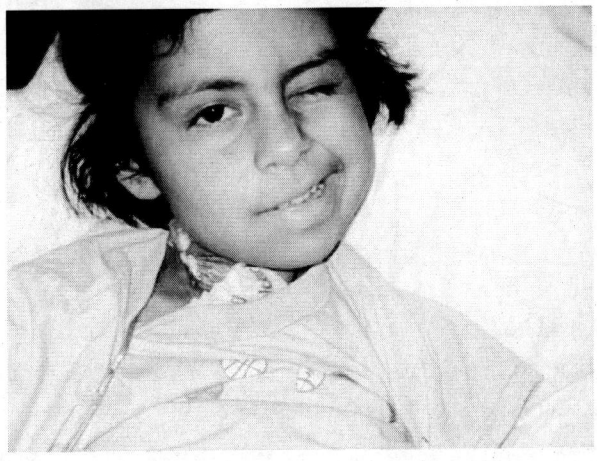

My girl, Kadesha winks at me.

27 May 2007

Dear family and friends,

It is eighteen minutes after midnight and I cannot sleep again. Some nights are like that. Noise from outside is keeping me awake. My mind is racing with thoughts of the day.

Earlier I had walked through the Intensive Care Unit (ICU) of the 47th Combat Support Hospital, Mosul, Iraq, where I work. A new patient has arrived, lying with his chest exposed and his vital signs electronically monitored. He is ill and we are taking care of him, but he is different than most of our patients. He lies in bed with a bandana covering his eyes, not a bandage. He wears the orange pants of a prisoner. At the foot of the bed are two young American soldiers with weapons in hand. They look at me as I look at our patient, a "bad guy" for sure, as our Iraqi interpreter calls them. He is an insurgent.

My blood pressure rises a bit. I ask, "What did he do?" The answer comes, "He made IEDs." IEDs are Improvised Explosive Devices, bombs which are hidden to explode on the unsuspecting. This man is a terrorist, an evil, mean man who plots to kill our folks, other Iraqis, even innocent young children. My blood pressure rises even more. Something inside me wants to walk up to this guy, blindfolded or not, and just clobber him. Perhaps I will remove the bandana, so he can see it coming. People certainly do not see the IEDs coming before they explode, destroying life, injuring arms, legs, and bodies.

I look down at this insurgent, an elderly, overweight man. I wonder how we can love our enemies, and how we can pray for those who spitefully use us. I have lived a life with no real enemies. Here is a man who would take my life if he could.

Hate and anger raged in me for a time. Other soldiers who see these men without the bandannas tell me that there is in some of them no light in their eyes, no hope, no goodness that you can see. They are filled with a vile fluid which cannot be easily drained. They are cold and given the chance would do us harm.

As I walk through the Emergency Department (ED) there are often young American soldiers lying there, injured and receiving care. Twice this week I asked what happened and the answer was the same: an IED had hit their vehicles. No one was hurt badly—not these times—but there were injuries and the vehicles were badly damaged. How often this happens when I do not walk by, I do not know. I do not work in the ED often.

From the ICU I walk onto the ward. The staff is glad to see me. One of the children who arrived during a mass casualty a couple of weeks ago is having new problems. A mass casualty is when many patients are injured at once and are brought to the hospital at the same time. On that occasion two weeks ago, an insurgent drove his truck into a marketplace advertising discounted food and free flour to the local folks. The children were playing and families gathered and then the truck exploded, killing about 30 people and injuring over 70. Twenty-five of the more seriously wounded were brought to our hospital. Twelve of them were young children. I still remember the bleeding, broken bones, head injuries and a little girl with her intestines covered by a plastic bag.

I have been taking care of this little girl for almost two weeks. The explosion partially eviscerated or disemboweled her, but the medics covered the exposed bowel with a plastic bag, and our skilled surgeons sewed her back together. She smiles and waves at me now. She was excited to get crayons, a note pad and a candy bar earlier today. These items were sent freely for the giving by good Americans wanting to help.

The staff tells me she is having problems. Perhaps we should have suspected them earlier. The day before, she was not herself; she was not eating as well, and seemed to be uncomfortable. We did a CT scan that showed fluid below her wound; it didn't look particularly worrisome. She did not have a fever, and her vital signs were normal. Now her abdominal wound, where her intestines had once been blown out of her body by this truck-borne IED set off in the marketplace, is draining pus. The infection is from the dirty bomb fragments which entered her body. Now the infected fluid from her abdominal abscess is pouring through the stitches in her skin. The draining pus scares her and she is crying. It hurts as the nurses work on her and she cries more. I want to cry too.

My little girl had already had multiple surgeries. The surgeons took her back several times to clean out the wound, and again to close the open hole. She had been doing well, but now thick white pus drains across her belly and onto the bed. The nurses are cleaning it up. We send lab studies, a culture and a gram stain, hoping to identify this new microscopic enemy and provide the proper antibiotics to help her heal. This wound needs to drain. Incision and drainage are indicated. Her surgeon is called.

She will get better, but it will take more time. Her wounds will need to be cleaned and drained again. As time goes on perhaps the vileness and anger that we find in our enemies and ourselves will also drain away. This country needs more time to heal.

I sometimes eat lunch with some Iraqis who work with us, and listen to incredible stories of their struggles. They are trying to help with the healing. The infected need to be found; infected men like this insurgent laying in our ICU. They need to be drained from the society so that the healing can continue. When this man recovers from the illness that brought him to our ICU he will go to jail. That is where we keep the infected here, those infected with evil and hate. One of our doctors goes there every day to make sure they are healthy.

Perhaps this writing allows me to drain a bit as well. Perhaps I need to try to see this man as someone who is infected by the society in which he grew up, infected by the lies with which he was raised about life and about us, "the infidels" as he would call us. Infidels are those who are not of his faith, not of his country. The insurgents are taught the strictness of the law, but not taught mercy and compassion. They are taught that the worth of a man is nothing, but we know that the worth of man is great in the sight of God. All people have worth. I will try to forgive. I do not understand him, the man lying in the bed with the bandanna over his eyes; I don't think that I can. Perhaps he cannot understand either, cannot understand why we take care of his illness and do not return the hate and anger which he brings to us and makes us feel.

The rotors of a helicopter outside my living quarters roar gently and shake the walls. Things are happening out there in the middle of the night, as they do every day and night. I have talked to young soldiers whose job is to look for bombs, at least for now. Sometimes the bomb goes off and they are injured and brought into our ED. We are finding the bombs, the IEDs, lots of them, but not all of them. We are finding the men who make these IEDs and there will be fewer bombs, and lives will be saved. May the Lord bless those brave young men and women who put their lives on the line to stop the explosions and bring in the terrorists, the insurgents, the "bad men." This is my prayer tonight as I head back to bed to try to sleep, while the blades turn and the soldiers work.

MORE ON THE INSURGENT

"As in America, we do not want to punish the innocent, and here we certainly do not want to make an enemy of someone who would be your friend."

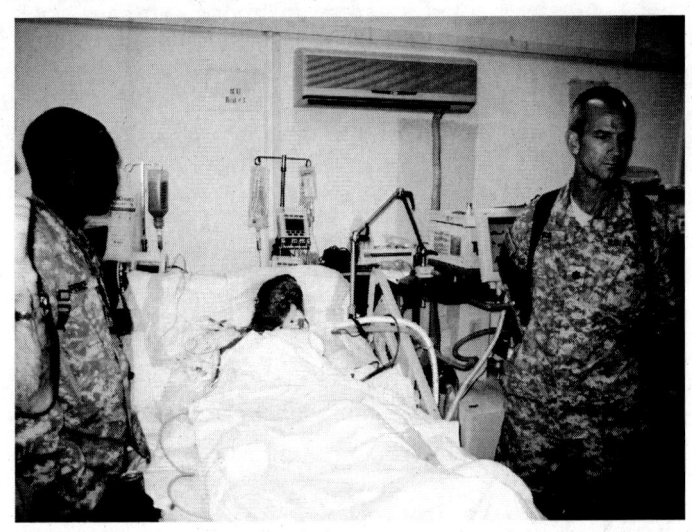

Doctors Alec Eror and Shawn Price round on an Iraqi patient who had been burned quite badly.

2 June 2006

Dear family and friends,

I thought that I would give you an update on the insurgent and how an experience with taking care of him has affected me. First, let me give a little update on life in Mosul for me.

Another week has gone by rather quickly. I am staying busy with lots of things. As usual for me, there still is not enough time to do everything I would like to do. I started each day this week before 5:00 with a 6 mile run. Most soldiers are required to start the day with PT, Physical Training, to include calisthenics and running. I want to try to keep up with them. Early in the morning is the only time when the temperature is not like standing in front of an oven door, recently opened. It has been up to 110 degrees. The sun is not up yet, but it is light enough to see, and yes, I run in a safe place, along the "berm," the edge of the base which has high obstructive fences and guards.

After finishing my run, I then shower and eat breakfast, often a box of cereal with a box of European type milk and have a piece of fruit.

It is then off to the hospital to see the inpatients I follow before morning rounds. I feel like an intern again, gathering numbers and presenting patients to the team. Notes are done early and then after rounds I have been working in the outpatient clinic until lunch. Some days when it has slowed down I get a bit of reading in. After lunch I return for more clinic, but it is done early in the afternoon, so I check on my patients, and do some more reading. I am trying to get ready for recertifying in pediatrics and peds heme/onc when I get back in October. Each day I read in the Old Testament with a plan to finish it before I leave. There have been other things to attend, Church on Sunday, scripture study on Thursday night, a farewell for one of the interpreters who is leaving in a week, a concert of a pretty good active duty band, an awards ceremony, the gym twice a week (I am working on getting buff) and a time to socialize outside my living quarters in the evening with several friends. Many have a cigar and I try to sit upwind to avoid the smoke. That is life at the forward operating base [FOB] for me.

Our terrorist has taken a turn for the worse. He has needed to be put on a ventilator. He is an older man, somewhat overweight with heart problems. I can tell you that our Iraqi interpreters hold no kindness for him and what he has done. One of them, a lady, commented very sarcastically, here is the "sexiest man in the world," as he lay smoking a white tube (intubated) with IVs in his arm, restraints, a blindfold and nothing else on but a loin cloth. One day as I walked through the ICU the nurses were bagging him. The pressures on the ventilator went up and he was having problems. I stopped to see if I could help. They had already called for a chest X-ray. I examined him and he was doing, at best, fair. The X-ray developer was not working. He seemed to have plugged his ET tube clinically, so I had them flush about 15 milliliters of saline down the tube. No, I was not trying to drown him. He sputtered and coughed up an ugly mucous plug, and then did much better as his airway was now open. I relate this to say that one time this man disgusted me and later I was literally helping to save his life. I felt that it was the right thing to do and was glad when he improved. It is a bit ironic.

Two days later as I came by, he again was having problems with his blood pressure and again I stopped and helped take care of him. It was good for me, for now I see him just as an ill patient and the hate and anger I had once felt for him are gone.

Many of the prisoners, who are ill and deemed to be just bad guys, are let go after being in the hospital, with a slap on the hand, so to speak. If they are deemed to be a "bad, bad" guy they are not let go, but may end up in Abu Ghraib or another prison, which is where he will go if he ever recovers. Determining them to be a truly dangerous insurgent is not an easy thing. Also, returning them to their communities if they are determined to not be dangerous is not easy. As in America, we do not want to punish the innocent, and here we certainly do not want to make an enemy of someone who would be your friend. On the other hand we do not want to send someone back to the community only to have them set another bomb or shoot a rifle at you at some future time.

Good news. The two pediatric patients who remain in the hospital from the first big market place explosion and mass-cal are doing better and may be discharged in the next day or two. The little 6-year old girl's abscess has quit draining and the wound is clear. She is eating and we took her to a concert Wednesday night. The 101st band was playing music of all kinds, including some great rock and roll. She really enjoyed the music. You could see it in her dark eyes and in the smile on her beautiful face. She first waved her hands, then stood and soon was dancing. Pictures were flashing. She was a highlight of the evening.

Another 12-year old boy, who lost his hand and arm below the elbow and foot just above the ankle in an explosion set off by an insurgent, has been really struggling. His uncle spent about two weeks with him, but has six kids of his own and had to leave over a week ago. He was a nice man. The poor young boy just cried and cried when he was left alone and he begs to go home. He has regressed a lot, as he needs pretty much total care, but he is progressing. His own parents have not been able to make it here as of yet. There is work, other kids to take care of and travel is difficult. He wants to go home so badly. He has dressings on his new skin graft which are supposed to come off tomorrow and if okay, will be out the door soon. He has a lot of recovery left. It is hard to use crutches to walk with the missing foot when you have no hand on the same side to hold a crutch. Just getting up in bed is a huge struggle. Our physical therapists have made a special crutch he can use. It is tied onto his forearm stump and braced by his upper arm. It was amazing to see him taking his first steps. Like a 10-months old child he carefully stepped out, one step at a time, a hop with the crutch and then another step. He was given hope for improvement and you could see that hope in his eyes.

He also attended the concert and for the first time had a real smile on his face. He got his share of pictures taken of him. With his wounds, folks feel more for him. Both he and Kadesha are very lucky to be alive, I assure you. He loves to play the Tetris game I gave him, though he really can't do it with only one hand, but I don't think he really knows how it is supposed to work and neither does he care. It is an American toy and he is pleased.

We had a US soldier shot in Mosul by a sniper, a highly trained sharpshooter. When this happens I am sickened and hate to think of the family waiting and praying for him. We had another young soldier in his twenties die after leaving the gym. He had a heart attack. He had pill fragments of body building supplements in his stomach. Eighteen different supplements were later found in his living quarters in large quantities, enough to fill a small suitcase. They are not good. I ask every soldier in the clinic if they are taking supplements. Many have, but it seems that some will often not admit it if they are.

Things in Mosul and here are much quieter than in Baghdad or Balad. We see fewer patients by quite a bit. Both places are terrible because Iraqis are killing Iraqis and us if they can. As the weather has warmed up, so has the terrorist activity.

I appreciate your prayers and notes. Many of you know that my daughter Kaylene was in an accident last Sunday. I am so thankful that she is okay. The concern for family and friends does not go away just because you are half way across the world. My prayers are with each of you as well. Well, that is it for today. I hope this is reaching each of you. Some have responded so at least for some, this is getting through and your notes are getting back to me.

A GOOD DAY IN IRAQ—A TRUE FATHER'S DAY STORY

"He appreciated the gift of life that she was given, and the life which will continue in his family, in spite of those who would take it away."

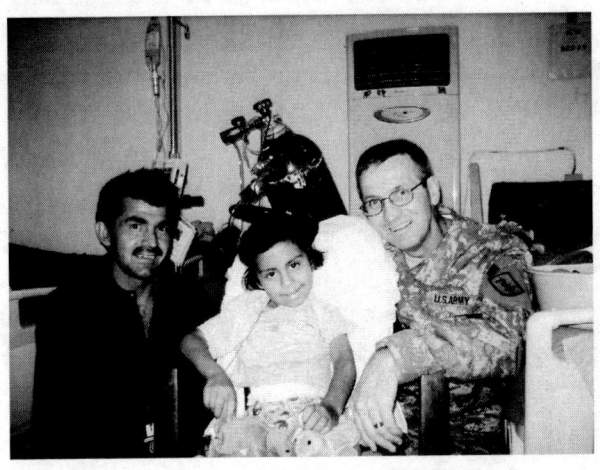

Kadesha, her father and myself as she recovered.

10 June 2006

Dear family and friends,

Tuesday was a good day in Iraq for a little girl and her family. Six-year old Kadesha left the 47th Combat Support Hospital (CSH) in Mosul, Iraq, after four weeks. She went home with her father. She was originally brought in with 11 other children, after an IED exploded in a marketplace.

After the blast, our troops swept into this dangerous location. When one IED goes off, another may be near by. The medics gave first aid and began transferring the most injured. Wounds were mended and hope was given.

When Kadesha was brought in, many other patients, including child after child, came in on stretchers. I was both amazed and horrified. She had a plastic bag over her abdomen covering her bowels. I thought to myself, "This little girl is a dead girl." Immediately the surgery team took her to the operating room to begin a heroic rescue. A breathing tube and IV's were placed, and life saving blood started.

LTC Thomas Curry, a vascular surgeon from Tripler Army Medical Center, was the head surgeon. Skillful hands sewed her bowels back together. The skin over the wound was partially gone and very injured. Healing would be difficult.

In the Intensive Care Unit there were fluid, nutrition and breathing issues. Medicines for pain, sedation, and infection were administered. Each day, MAJ Alexander Niven, a critical care specialist from Madigan Army Medical Center, skillfully reviewed system by system.

She began to recover, but she was alone. In the community, families waited. In many cases they did not know if loved ones survived or not. Our social worker tried to contact their families. Kadesha's parents were one of the few contacted.

Kadesha's mother, dressed in a hijab and abaya, the cultural dress of the area, entered the ICU. You could only see her eyes. Nevertheless, you could see that she was a beautiful woman with a good heart. When she first set her eyes on her very sick little girl, she could not contain herself. Tears, which could not be hidden, flowed profusely from her dark eyes and down her cheeks.

With some fear and trepidation, she held first the hand and then the little face and gently kissed Kadesha. The mother and child were reunited and Kadesha's eyes reached longingly out to her mother, though her arms could not. It took some time for the tenderness of the scene to fade, and I hope that it will never fade from my memory.

After a time this kind woman then went to see the other children. I remember the recognition in her eyes. They were obviously from her neighborhood. They were in hospital beds with bones and wounds mended, and they were alone. Some of their parents surely did not know if they were yet alive. Many from the blast were not. Kadesha's mother would have good news.

The mother's visit passed rather quickly. The next day, Kadesha's father came. He was able to stay at her bedside from that day until this. I think the culture and the needs of the family prohibited the mother from staying. This caring father showed what it means to be a dad, encouraging his daughter to eat, to move, to take her respiratory treatments. He helped her through several additional surgeries.

This good man would communicate, not through words,

but through his body language how grateful he was for what the team did. He spoke often with his hand over his heart, as is the custom here, meaning his words came from the heart. He learned the words, "Thank You." Each day, covering his heart, he would thank those who took care of his daughter.

Kadesha healed and began to blossom. The 101st Division band put on a concert. Kadesha was allowed to attend and enjoyed the music. First she smiled, then following the crowd she raised her hands and waved back and forth. Later she stood with the good nurses and danced and danced. Her little hips moved as her arms swayed. When we saw her dancing, it was clear she was going to be fine. The band was good, very good, but she was the hit of the night.

Kadesha was showered with toys, stuffed animals, coloring books and a DVD player. For each item her father responded, "Thank you." She brought a different atmosphere into the hospital. She may leave a bit spoiled, but she made us remember our children and the tremendous value of a child to us and to a father. She is lucky to be alive and I am lucky to have seen the compassion of the team, and the tenderness of a father.

The other children injured by this first inexplicable act of terrorism have all gone home. From another tragedy we had yet another boy who was shot in the hand and had to have it amputated. He had been in the hospital for some time and also got to go home this week. His father had also been at his bedside, vigilant and helping. This boy's mother had been killed by insurgents the day he was injured, leaving his father to care for him. They had been involved in another war scene. Insurgents burst into their home trying to avoid a capture by Iraqi police, and small arms fire rang out in a small battle. It took much time for the boy to warm up, but he did and his father was so thankful that we could help save the life of his young son. The fathers taught the same lesson, the importance of being there for your child. Now it was Kadesha's day to go.

Since the first explosion and mass casualty, one of our life saving medics has given his own life as he served these people. He left a young wife and a small child. He was here to help, but a terrorist intervened. He was doing his duty and was hit by a sniper's rifle fire.

Soon it will be Father's Day and I will remember and be thankful for my own good father. I will remember the young medic lifesaver whose child will be without a father, and whose father will be without a son. I will pray for his wife, daughter and family. I am thankful for lives he saved.

I will also remember the example of Kadesha's father. I thank him for reminding us that we should be there for our kids. He loved his daughter and did what he could for her. He helped her heal as much as anything else that happened. He was ever at her side.

These fathers appreciated the gift of life that their children were given, and the life which will continue in their families, in spite of those who would take it away. Each became a friend, though we could not share much more than a strong hand shake, a hand across the heart, and the words, "Thank you."

MEDICAL CARE IN IRAQ

"Many Iraqi physicians left Mosul before we Americans came. Many others have gone now because they have become targets for violence."

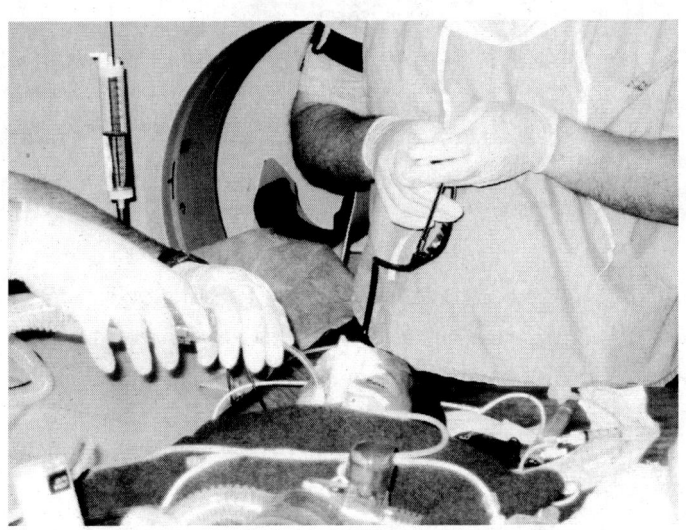

An injured Iraqi child prepares to go into the CT Scanner.

18 June 2006

Dear family and friends,

It was Wednesday night and I had gone to bed hoping for a good night's sleep. After just getting to sleep the dreaded sound of the pager startled me and I was suddenly very awake. The pager said that a child was in route and it was time to report to the hospital.

Somehow I was dressed and heading out the door. A Stryker unit showed up shortly thereafter with a child on a gurney. Right away you knew the airway was intact. The strong sound of the child's cry reassured us that there were no breathing problems. There was a large bandage on the child's head. This was worrisome.

The child was stripped down to look for other wounds. He was still wearing a diaper so I surmised that he must have been less than 3 years old. A nurse skillfully started a great IV on the first try and fluids were started. No other wounds were found. "What was the story?" I wondered.

This child had gone out in the night and chased after a Stryker, a sort of a tank on wheels. Before the soldiers could stop, the protective metal bumpers had hit the child on the head. They stopped and administered first aid and the child was taken to a local hospital by the parents. A plain film or x-ray showed no skull fracture and the wound was sewn shut. The Stryker leader recommended that the child be brought to the CSH for a more complete evaluation.

The parents arrived with the child. They stated that the Strykers were known to throw candy and gifts to the kids, and their child had gone into the street before they could stop him. The Strykers have stopped this practice because of just this sort of thing. They now go into the community or schools before they give out gifts which have been donated to the people of Iraq as tokens of good will.

A blow to the head could mean a much more serious injury. The child was taken to the CT scanner. At the last mass cal, a slightly older girl had been hit in the head and though she looked good at first, her level of consciousness dropped. Her CT showed bleeding in her head, so she was sent to Balad where we have a neurosurgeon. Unfortunately, we got news that she did not make it.

Fortunately for this child, the CT was completely normal. Corbin Partridge, a head and neck surgeon, noted that the wound was not closed to our standard. We asked the family about taking the child to the OR for better closure. Without this, he would likely have an unsightly scar later on. The family agreed. The wound was noted to be clear to the skull, and have some hair and dirt left inside when it was washed out. This had been the right recommendation.

The family was very grateful for the concern and care given their child. They were quite amazed at the number of physicians who paid attention to their child and the level of care provided to them. In the community hospital, they said that a single physician worked and that he was not very good. He was very busy with many patients. I told them that I was sure he was doing the very best that he could with the things that he had, and we were lucky to have such a group of talented physicians.

One of our interpreters is a retired physician from Mosul. He left Iraq and moved to Syria in 1997. Work here was nearly impossible. He was not part of the elite group, and did not support Saddam. He was paid about $3.00 a day for his services. He can now make more as an interpreter than as a physician and it is safer. He thinks that a physician here gets about $2–3000 a month, but often the people do not have money to pay. The physicians are paid by the government. A grade school teacher got $10 a month under Saddam. A college professor may get $1000 a month.

We have had an Iraqi physician come to our hospital. He is a good and intelligent man, but lacks the equipment and resources that he needs to take care of the patients he has.

Many physicians left Mosul before we Americans came. Many others have gone now because they have become targets for violence. They are at risk to be bombed or kidnapped because of their great worth to the community. This leaves the people without access to good medical care. The educated, such as teachers, are also targets.

The people here are poor, though the country brings in much money from the oil wells. The wealth does not trickle down. The farming here that I can see is much like my dad who was a farmer described from 70 years ago in the states. Their fields are small, checker boarded with dikes. They irrigate them one at a time. I see where they cut the winter wheat and stack it in small piles around the field as happened years ago before farm equipment was available and the harvest had to be done by hand. I do see a few small bales in one field.

One farmer drives an old pickup and I could see him hauling a cow in the back. He is lucky. I understand that until recently only about 1 in 10 had cars. Someone thought that it is now 1 in 3 adults with cars. Flushing toilets are not common. Some would not know how to use them. They have a hole in the floor and they squat. Paper is not used. It is an offense to offer someone your left hand. You might guess why.

With more freedom and the ability to use the technology such as is available in the US, this country could really blossom like a beautiful rose. Perhaps that is part of the reason we are here, to not only bring freedom, but also to help the people move forward. I have not been out to really see the country, but I can see glimpses as they come through the hospital. Certainly, seeing the living conditions here and what we have, makes one realize that we are very blessed compared to the large majority of people in the world. It makes one wonder why we are so blessed, and wonder "what is our responsibility to the peoples of the world?"

Today I am thankful that we could help a little boy who was in an accident. I feel for the people here who do not have the medical resources that we have. I am also thankful for the doctor in Mosul, who I have not met, but who is doing the best that he can to help his people in very difficult and dangerous circumstances.

FIELD OF DREAMS

"We must learn what God would have us learn now through life's challenges. One thing we must learn is to simply have faith and trust in God, as a child has trust in his parent."

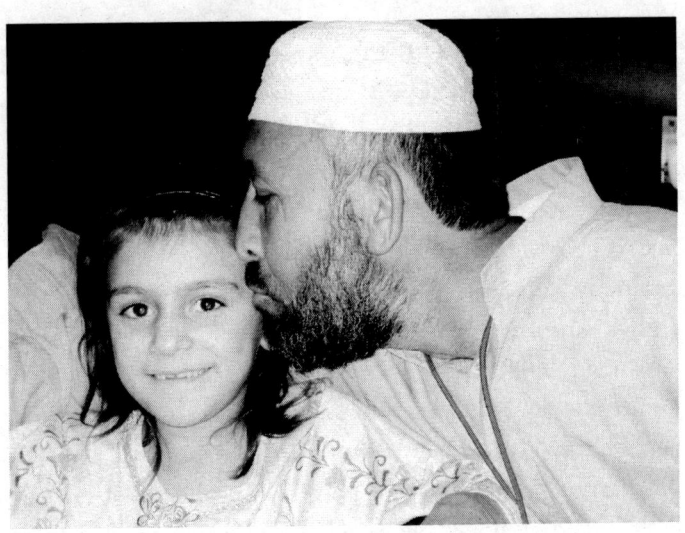

In the hospital an Iraqi father kisses his daughter.

24 June 2006

Dear family and friends,

Last Sunday was Father's Day. I got to talk to my children. I also talked to Dad, as I try to do each week. Wednesday was my daughters', Allyson and Kaylene's, birthday, so I talked to them again. They are exactly two years apart and share the same birthday. It was a great week. I also got to talk to my son Garrett. My other son, Jordan, sent a nice message, though it did not come to my e-mail, but my wife, Sharon, read it to me. He is in Bolivia and I can not talk to him.

I received many boxes from many of you and others. These contain things for the people here and I am working to get them out to the people, including the children. Thank you for your generosity on behalf of our country.

I had the opportunity this week to talk about life, death and God with a friend of mine. He read the note I sent last week about the child whose head was hit by a military vehicle (and who fortunately did fine), and asked, "What would you have told the parents had the child not done fine, if he had been killed?"

In my work, I have had the occasion to talk to many parents about similar questions. As a pediatric oncologist I work with many children diagnosed with cancer. Some of them do not make it. This question is one of the great questions people ask, "Why do bad things happen to good people?" The inquiry could easily be posed with other slants, "Why is there bad or evil in the world, if God is good?" "Why did this happen to me, or to my child, or my family?" "Why are things so unfair?" "Why did this happen—death or sickness—to my child and not instead to me?"

These are the hard questions, and I do not necessarily have the answers. An attempt at the answer is not easily given, nor understood by myself, nor by most people. Sometimes the only thing we can say is, "I really don't know, but I do feel bad for you and for what has happened." Often the best we can do is to cry a tear, hold a hand, give a hug and say "I am so sorry, sorry for your loss, sorry for your pain. Because I also cared, because I also loved your child, it also hurts me to have seen this happen."

There is no answer which can bring back a departed child to parents who loved them so much. There is no good answer when there is an empty place at the dinner table or a bed which is not disturbed by the peaceful sleep of a loved child. The world is often empty for these parents and families. That empty hole never fully goes away and we hold onto it because of love. They do learn through these great tribulations. They are changed.

I recall my own good mother, about 40 years after the loss of her son, my brother Myron. He was just 5 years old (I was one year old) and he was hit by a car and taken from us. He was in Kindergarten. Mom had purchased a cap gun for him, but bought no caps. He wanted to get them so badly, that he ran to the store before school started, with a little dime clenched in his hand. From the store he ran, heading back to school before it started. Out between two parked cars and into the street he ran, where he was hit by a high school student who could not stop in time, and immediately was killed.

Forty years later as mother told the story, with great tears in her eyes and pain in her voice she cried, as if it had just happened, "If I had only bought him the caps." She carried that burden, which she could not let go of, because she loved him so much. You see, the pain will never completely go away for a parent who loses a child, because the love will never go away, neither in this life nor in the next. That love is something we will take along with us. Love lasts forever.

I told my friend in brief what I would tell that mother, as I have told many mothers and fathers before; that they will never stop loving their child. They will never stop missing him or her, nor completely stop hurting from the loss.

There is some hope and promise in believing some things. I tell people who ask that I believe with all my heart and feel that it is true that the child does not cease to exist. The child, now as a real personage of spirit, will still be the same in personality. Their child will continue to be an individual who is conscious, intelligent, and who loves them, and is able to learn, and to think and to do certain things in a spiritual state. I explain that the spirit is that which gives our body life and when the body dies, it does not mean that the spirit dies as well. In fact there is good evidence to the contrary, but we must have faith to believe. The spirit gives our body life, as our hand gives a glove life, but the glove is just the shell of the real life that is there.

I recall talking at the funeral of one little boy who died of a brain tumor. His name was Nicco, and he loved dinosaurs. He loved them with all his heart. He carried books about them and knew their names, and had toy dinosaurs to comfort him. As I talked, it hit me that perhaps this little spirit was greeted, comforted, loved and held by the Savior Jesus Christ, and by others who loved him. With God's arms around Nicco, perhaps he heard something like this, "I love

you so much Nicco. I have something I want to show you."
Perhaps in some far off corner of the universe is a world
which is covered with real living dinosaurs, even now. "Nicco,
I have a place you can visit where you can be with the dinosaurs, a real Jurassic Park. You will love to see and visit this
place, but you also have a warm, safe home with me, where
you will live. There will be no needles, no chemo, no pain,
and no fear there."

"At some short time, your parents will come to be with you,
one at a time, and you will be able to teach them things you
learn here. You will be able to take them to see the dinosaurs.
You will be able to know, love and be with them for thousands
and millions of years. It will not be a long wait for you, though
to your parents the wait will seem very long indeed." Eternity
is forever, billions of years and more, and earth life, which
seems so long, is really nothing in comparison.

Earth life is not fair, but God's love will make up for the
losses, and we can have faith and hope in that. The love will
never end, for we never end. Nicco's parents will see him
again and will know him. Perhaps part of his job there in
heaven is to be a guardian angel for his parents, or for his
sisters. My mother who has recently died, I am sure, is reac-
quainted with my brother Myron, her little boy. The love
never ends. The relationship never ends. Nicco will always
be their son, and they will always be his parents.

To really understand this, we talked of the hope that we
can have. My friend and I talked of the rest of the story;
where we came from, who we are, who God our Father
in Heaven is, and who Jesus Christ is and how there is a
plan. We talked of the purposes of life which is in part to

have joy, to serve, to prepare for life after we are gone from mortality. We talked of the requirements of faith and giving one's heart to God for Eternal Life, which is life with God and with our loved ones forever.

He asked many questions and we talked for a good time. He asked an interesting question, in effect, "If your father dies as an old man, and you died as a young man, and a child dies, what age will they be and what will they look like?" I replied that I believe the old man and the young man would be the same age, in the prime of their lives. They would be resurrected in glorified and perfected bodies, but that they would know each other well and the "age" would mean nothing. I said that many believe that the parents will get to raise a small child who dies to adulthood, and that seemed right to me.

As our discussion ended he replied, "You have an answer for everything." I said that there should be answers. But, I also said that I do not have an answer for everything, not even for most things, but I do have hope and believe in God, his goodness, forgiveness and blessings for us in his greater plan. There are good answers for us to learn.

At church last week, as the speakers talked about fathers and Father's Day, one talked about how he enjoyed throwing a ball with his father, but that his dad was often too busy, and how he always made sure that he wasn't too busy to do the same with his son.

The movie *Field of Dreams* came to mind. Perhaps this is one of the best Father's Day stories out there. Kevin Costner played the part as the son, and through the miracle of the field, he was able to know his father again, both men in their prime, and both men feeling the love which would not go away, as they threw a ball to each other. That evening as I went to call Sharon and the kids, by the Lord's tender mercy, the same movie, *Field of Dreams*, was on at the MWR–Morale, Welfare and Recreation center (where I make the phone call). I thought of the great truth the movie tells and the answer which was there, but missed by so many. I was touched as I watched.

I thought of this and my earlier conversation with my friend. I thought, "We must trust in God's goodness, his mercy, and his compassion. We must trust in more than this life and its hard questions. We must trust in eternity, and in family. We must learn what God would have us learn now through life's challenges. One thing we must learn is to simply have faith and trust in God, as a child has trust in his parent." I hope my friend will keep asking questions. His questions teach me also. How can we learn without questions?

May the Lord bless each of you in all you do, especially all who are dealing with health problems and other challenges. I send my love to each of you, to my wonderful family and good friends. Thanks so much.

INDEPENDENCE DAY

"The flag represents more than home, it represents my country. It represents freedom and the good which our country stands for."

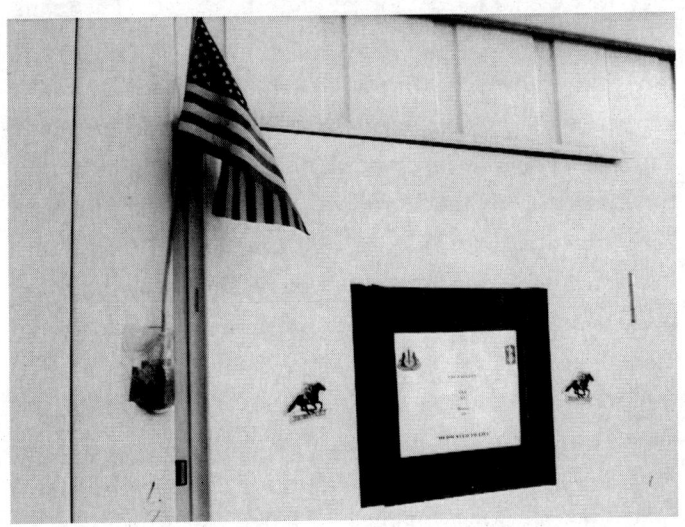

The small American flag outside my door.

1 July 2006

Dear family and friends,

Last night it was my turn to cover the Emergency Department. Fortunately, I do not have a heart wrenching story to tell. Things were relatively quiet from the time I started my coverage early in the evening until the enlisted had their change of shift. We had a few cases, but nothing too interesting or serious. We had a bit of time for some teaching but there were no patients waiting at 11:00 PM, so I headed to bed, with my pager ready to call me back in case someone came in.

As I went to my Containerized Housing Unit, CHU, as they are called, I looked for my door in the dark. The rooms are about the size of the back of a bobtail moving truck. In fact, that is how they were build and brought in. They have neither running water nor restroom, but they do have light and thank goodness, air conditioning. They are home for the time, and they are much better than the tents they used earlier in the war and which are still being used in other places. We are not allowed to build permanent structures for our soldiers in Iraq according to our agreement with the government. The CHUs stand in a long row and mine is #10. The way I know which door is mine is by a small American flag which is flying attached to a 24-inch dowel above my doorpost. There are no lights outside the CHUs. In the dark, I slowly moved forward looking for that small flag. When I get to the flag, I know that I am home.

The thought crossed my mind, as the 4th of July was coming, that this was a very symbolic thing for me. I have always been a supporter of the flag and the country it stands for. The next time I step on American soil, with a large flag flying over it, I will once again be home, whether this happens in Texas, Washington or somewhere else. The flag represents home. The flag represents more than home, it represents my country. It represents freedom and the good which our country stands for.

There have been wars fought to protect that freedom and to preserve it. The flag has changed since it was first flown over the colonies, who declared themselves free and independent. A war had to be fought to win that freedom. Another terrible war was fought to preserve the union of our country and to insure that its freedoms were applied to all people. The flag has been hoisted in many other countries as we fought around the world to protect that freedom.

Perhaps one of the most famous flag raisings happened on Iwo Jima, Japan, during WW II. We invaded an island fortress and with the loss of thousands of lives we finally took the island. It is interesting that Iwo Jima is not now American soil. When we raised a flag there, it was a symbol of our determination to preserve our freedom, to fight on, to win, and the men who saw the flag raised that day cheered. Many of them did not make it home as the fighting was not over. Many were buried on that small island in the Pacific. The flag was not a symbol of colonization and conquest there, nor in Germany, nor in Korea.

A few short years ago we came to Iraq for the second time. Within a short time our troops were in control and in their enthusiasm raised an American flag over this country. This was very quickly taken down and the Iraqi flag put up instead. It was neither our intention to conquer this country and to make it American soil, nor to colonize and expand our borders. It was our goal to help this country, and the whole of the Middle East move more toward freedom and to put down terrorism and absolute power. It was our plan to help give these people some of the freedoms which we enjoy and thus help preserve our own freedom.

There may have been many reasons weighed in the equation to come here. I do not have enough political understanding to know how each was considered. There were rumors or reported evidence of weapons of mass destruction. There is the possible issue of unfinished business from former presidencies. There is oil here, and we are big oil consumers. I don't know about the validity of these reasons, but I do know from what I have seen some other things.

I know that there had been suppression, abuse of power, murder, genocide, and fear in this country. I know that the people did not have the freedoms we enjoy. I know that many lacked hope and that the wealth and power were garnered by a few, while the majority of the country went without. They did not see any potential change in their future, no hope, no chance for education, progress or for freedom. I don't know if this is partly why we came, but it should be why we, and those of the unified coalition, fight while we are here, and one could argue, why we should stay.

Should this country be our business? We certainly have our own set of problems back home. We could use the massive amount of money spent here to build and strengthen our own people and communities. Nevertheless these people are human beings with whom we share the globe. Do we or can we see beyond our own borders?

I think of the small flag flying outside my CHU. I think

of the larger ones flying back over American soil. I think of the things they stand for; inalienable rights, life, liberty and the pursuit of happiness. I think of one nation under God, indivisible, with liberty and justice for all. I feel that those are good principles and that we have some responsibility as people and as a country which enjoys these rights.

When I was a teenager, before I really considered joining the military, I was told that my mission in life would not be in foreign countries, but in my own. I joined the military to help get an education, which I could not otherwise afford. I did not plan on staying in. That was 26 years ago and I have worn the uniform of the United States Army since then. I have served our country in some degree caring for the children of the fighting men and women. This really is my first tour overseas and I see that here I can continue my mission for our country. Most of the people I take care of on a day to day basis are Iraqi. Perhaps I can be an ambassador for our country, and for the freedoms, rights and blessings we enjoy under the American Flag.

I have served as a leader with the Boy Scouts of America for about 15 years. I have taught the boys to respect the flag, to fold it, and to do their duty to God and to their country. I am glad that I have been able to do my duty to my country as well.

On this Fourth of July, when the fireworks go off all over our country, let us remember the hope and freedom that those lights represent. Let us remember the lives which have been lost to preserve that freedom for ourselves and for the peoples of this earth. Because of the sacrifice of so many, there is freedom where our young soldiers gave their lives, in Gettysburg, Japan, Germany, France and Korea and many places around the world. In many of these places the U.S. flags that still occasionally fly there are over the graves of the American soldiers who died there and never returned home. These foreign soils became their final resting places. The only soil we took was that we used to bury our dead who sacrificed to make their countries safe and free. There were once kings, emperors, dictators and tyrants ruling these countries and now the people who live in those places have freedom. I am so very thankful for our veterans, both living and dead, who served selflessly to defend our country and the peoples of the world.

Let us remember the flag and what it stands for. We should stand up when it goes by, and at attention salute or put our hand on our heart and say thanks for the blessings and freedoms we have. Let us recognize that other people of the world also desire those same blessings. Lastly, I hope that we really enjoy a good hot dog or hamburger, perhaps a lemonade and a parade, family and friends and really enjoy being Americans.

UNDER FIRE

"There were wars and killings going on before we came here. There is still much fighting among the different factions."

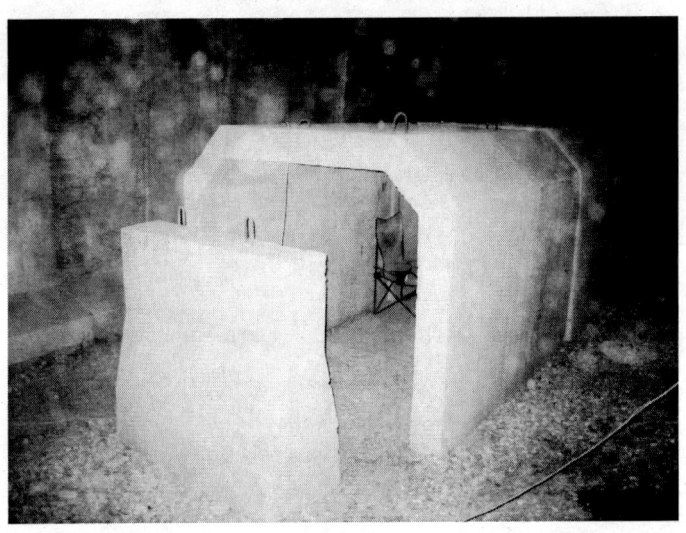

The bunker outside our living quarters.

9 July 2006

Dear family and friends,

Hello from Mosul. I am well and time is passing relatively fast. I feel extremely safe here, though there are bad things which could happen. Occasionally, about once a week, we are called to take cover in the bunkers or hear a large explosion and take cover. You sit and try to chat, try to make small talk, to laugh, and to visit. If the blasts continue everyone is soon silent, somber, waiting and I am sure offering silent prayers. Your heart is racing and your thoughts drift back home to family or to the hospital and the chance for potential injured. We sit huddled together, some in their battle rattle with Kevlar helmets and vests while others are in a t-shirt and shorts. We wait for the all clear call and then subdued chatter resumes and life gradually returns to normal. We do not get mortared often, compared to earlier. LTC Donald McClellan, who was here a year ago as a physician, said that they were often mortared daily for weeks at a time.

A week ago we had several mortars hit the FOB (Forward Operating Base). This is the first time in a long time that they hit the base. I was running at the time and was further away from the blast than if I would have been in my CHU or at the hospital. We heard one blast, then another and another and yet another. I was running with a couple of other people and we wondered if we should hit the bunkers. We were heading toward the blasts, we slowed down and the shooting stopped. As we got closer to the prison, there was a small column of smoke, which is where one round went off. One dud, which failed to detonate, was found nearby as well. Later I inspected the site and one of the blasts had blown through the corner of a CHU, but the occupant was on leave and not there at the time. Had he been there he easily could have been killed.

We finished the run and went to the hospital as the call of the pager sounded shortly after we heard the last blast. American soldiers were changing shift near the prison entrance and five were injured and brought to the hospital. I headed the trauma team for one who had four pieces of shrapnel in his body. One was very near his carotid artery, the others in his arm and back. Nothing was broken and his head was okay with no internal bleeding. He was really upset at the whole thing; "pissed" was the word he used over and over. He had been out on convoys for most of the 10 months he had been here and had recently been assigned to the FOB where he thought he would be safe. He had about six weeks to finish his tour. He was in the wrong place at the wrong time and was not happy to think that he was now injured. All of the soldiers did okay. Fortunately there were no serious injuries. It was more of a nuisance for them than anything else.

Over the last month we have lost 4 soldiers in Mosul, about one a week, from apparent sniper activity. I hope that they can get the guy who is doing this. I hate to think of the soldiers' families getting the news. One was a new lieutenant who had just been in country for about two weeks. One was about ready to go home in a month. One was a medic from Oregon who left a wife and a little girl. My heart goes out to them.

On the FOB a few weeks ago a young soldier was heading to the gym when he heard something and suddenly felt a pain in his back. After a few steps he had to go to his knees. Two of the CSH nurses came by and stopped to see what the problem was. They noted blood on his back and called for help, and then assisted in getting him to the hospital. He did okay after a short stay in the hospital. From where he was located at the time, one would surmise that this was a random shot into the FOB, shot from a long distance. The bullet was not American, so it was not fired by one of our guys. About the time he was hit the military police noted a breech in the perimeter and thus the base was under high alert for some time. This meant that we had to deal with extra ID checks, extra guards etc., but nothing else came of it.

Some of the soldiers are struggling. Since we have been here there has been a suicide and a couple of attempts. There is nothing much worse than one of our own soldiers taking their own life. We have a good psychiatrist and a good awareness of the risks here. Everything that can be done to prevent this is being done.

That said, the Americans have fared very well compared to the Iraqi people. There have been many deaths in the Iraqis that I have seen, from young children to older people. We have worked hard to save lives and been successful, but not all have made it in the end.

Overall there have been hundreds fewer trauma patients in the last year than in the years before, so that has been a very positive thing.

There were wars and killings going on before we came here. There is still much fighting between the different factions here. Some of the stories you read in the paper here are terrible. Some we still see firsthand.

This week, near Tal Afar another bomb went off. I believe that it was in a vehicle. The homicide bomber took many lives. I can't appropriately say suicide bombers when you think of what they do. Though they take their own lives, their main intent is to kill many other people at the same time. Thus I say they are homicide bombers. There were 48 wounded per our report. I am sure that we got the worst of the injured, those who were not killed. (I did not hear the report of the number killed.) We had only 9 come to the hospital, including three teen-aged boys. They were at a mosque on their Holy Day, which is Friday. They had gone to worship, when they were blindly attacked.

One bright teenage boy who was injured also had his glasses destroyed and so our optometrist made him a new pair. He was grateful that he could see clearly again. I hope that he can see the evils of militant Islam and the good that we are trying to bring to this country. He is a bright kid. Down the road I hope that he will not join in the retaliation, but in the building of his country and the world.

The shootings, the bombs, the killings often seem so random and the victims are most often innocent of any real crime, especially any war crimes. The purpose of these killings is not clear. Are they done only for hate? How does killing and injuring children and people praying at a mosque or shopping in a marketplace achieve any real political goal? These are questions one might ask as they look at fighting this war. Who and what are our enemies?

I am thankful that I feel safe, though there are sometimes bombs going off around me. I am thankful that there are fewer bombs, fewer mortars, fewer attacks than there were before. I am thankful that our enemies are bad shots in general and that we didn't have anyone hurt too badly this week when a mortar hit the FOB. I am thankful that we at least can understand why we shoot when we do. I hope that we will never fight nor kill for the wrong reasons. I am thankful that I am here to try to save and preserve life and that I do not, and have not had to shoot a weapon for any reason.

THANKS FOR YOUR SUPPORT

"There are many Iraqis here who are very grateful that we are here and for what has happened, and is happening in their country."

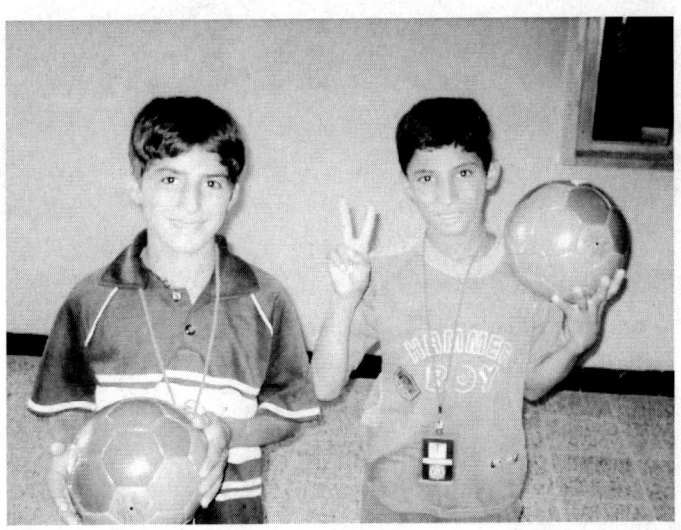

Two Iraqi boys smile as they get a soccer ball.

9 July 2006

Dear family and friends,

I wish to tell you how much I appreciate all that you and many others have done for me and for the people of Iraq. Many of you have contributed through sending boxes full of items for sharing. There have been soccer balls, clothes, candy, school items and hand held games, to name a few of the things I have received. It has been a way that people at home can feel a part in what is happening here. Thanks to you on behalf of those who have received your gifts here. (I am not soliciting more boxes, but wish to recognize those who have given.)

I have been able to share through the generosity of many people. More importantly than the material items, I have shared some hope and smiles, even if only in a small way. I have received around 30 packages, mostly from members of my church congregation back home, but also from others in the community. (By the end of my deployment I received 110 boxes.) I have received some from people who read my printed article. Writing is a way for me to share and sending items has been a way for some of you to share as well.

I have given diapers and wipes to a young boy whose spine was torn apart by bullets and who can not control his bladder and stool. The family has been very appreciative. Actually it is his uncle as this boy's parents were killed when he was injured as they tried to drive through a check point without stopping about a year ago. He was compassionately sent to a large hospital in the states for medical care, where he stayed for about six months. He is now walking, but having some drainage from one of his wounds which had been healed. It may be spinal fluid, so we are looking into this.

This boy is very sharp and learned some English while he was in the states. He has a niece who is about a year old and is failing to thrive. The uncle's eyes reach out and hope for help for his family. You can see that he is nearly over-whelmed. There are no products such as baby wipes in the Iraqi stores. These are such a luxury when we can get them.

I have been able to give soccer balls to a bunch of young boys and girls and to some fathers with children as they left the hospital. They are delighted with the gifts. (I have a small air pump to inflate them.) The large group of children who were injured in the last big bombing is coming back for follow-up, so each one leaves with some gifts and a soccer ball.

A beautiful, tall teenage girl, whose friends were killed in an attack on her car, came back for a procedure to straighten her legs. She did well. She likes to draw and was delighted with a drawing pad, pencils, and markers. She drew a nice picture for me of one of the Iraqi landmark buildings.

I have given some clothes such as girl's underwear to Kadesha when she came back, shirts to boys, etc. Boxes of school supplies, coloring books and crayons and toys have gone to the soldiers who are out in the Strykers and can stop and give them to the kids. One of the American groups has "adopted" a school and I was able to pass items on to them.

On the ward each day for a while I have taken the small candy bars which have been sent to me and passed them out, one to each patient, American and Iraqi. They seem so appre-ciative for such a small token, and often reply with heartfelt thanks. Today one of the Iraqi men had a box of candy and with a gleaming smile he passed them out to the doctors as we rounded. He was obviously glad that he could give as well.

We have literally saved many lives, saved many arms and legs and helped people recover. I have seen people with incredible burns and wounds who have been well taken care of. We have seen people sent from Iraqi hospitals where they had gotten worse and we have tried to fix their wounds. I have the opportunity here to work with an incredible group of physicians, nurses and with great hospital support people. We have made a good team and can provide some of the best care that can be received anywhere in the world.

Another positive thing has been the simple things that we have been able to do for individuals. There are many Iraqis here who are very grateful that we are here and for what has happened, and is happening in their country. There have been lives and hearts touched and lives saved. The country will be a better place, unless we just leave and let the insurgents feel that they have won. Victory for them will be that they outlasted us even if they accomplish nothing else.

Many would argue that we should not be here. Perhaps they are right in some aspects. Nevertheless we are here and since we are we can do some good. There are places like this all around the world, places which could use our help. The thing that makes me proud is that the American people, our churches and charities often are contributing here and in those places. They are giving and sharing regardless of color, nationality, religion or political background. People are all the same in what they want and need: family, freedom and the pursuit of happiness. I am glad to be part of that for a time.

May the Lord bless each of you. Thank you for your prayers, thoughts and friendship. Thank you again for your generosity on behalf of the Iraqi people.

GETTING OLDER

"Exercise is good for old folks, I think. I just don't understand why I get so sore so easily."

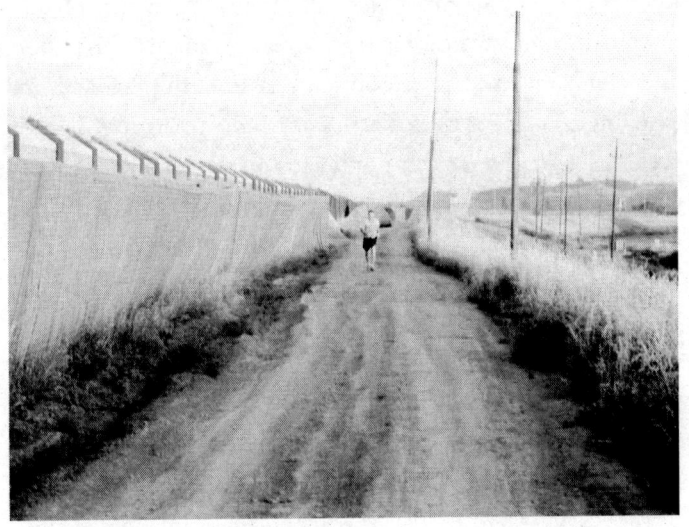

Running along the berm.

16 July 2006

Dear family and friends,

I turned 51 this week. I had a good birthday, as good as one could have away from home, in a country at war. I am now moving into the second half of my first century. I thought I would reflect on that just a bit.

Being 51 really makes me one of the older folks around here. Getting older is no fun really, and yet there are some good things which go with it. I am the senior COL at the CSH, and am senior to my 'bosses.' I am senior to COL Polo the hospital commander. (He has been a COL for two years; I have been for three.) I am senior to COL Stout, the DCCS (Deputy Commander for Clinical Services). That is okay with me, because having a break from administration and being involved in patient care is something that I am enjoying. As Chief of Pediatrics at Madigan Army Medical Center I sent seven other physicians on deployments as part of this war and I felt that it was my turn. After reviewing our options, I volunteered to come and be part of what is happening in the Army, and the slot was a clinical slot and not a leadership position. As I walk around the FOB my arm gets tired from saluting back as about everyone salutes me. That is good for old arms, I think.

I have been trying to do some exercise. Exercise is good for old folks, I think. I just don't understand why I get so sore so easily. Who has the Bengay? I have been able to run quite a bit, but there is one thing I don't understand. (Perhaps not being able to understand goes along with getting older.) I run just as hard as I did as a younger man, put in just as much energy, get even more tired and go so much slower. I personally think that any fast twitch muscle fibers I had have converted to something slower. Someone suggested this might be due to the increased weight I am carrying. Perhaps the slow twitch stuff weighs more. Anyway, speaking of weight, muscle weighs more than fat and I am sure that I have more muscle. I just don't understand why it needs so much extra padding to protect it.

I am otherwise doing okay. I still can see fine, and the line in the middle of my glasses, my bifocals, doesn't seem to bother me much any more. I can hear pretty well. Every night I hear the generator running and the air conditioner above my bed roaring on and off, but I don't notice it as much as I used to. Do you think the high decibel purr has anything to do with that?

Someone once told me that my teeth, weak when they came in due to a childhood infection and possibly drinking farm well water, would not last until thirty. I still have them, though they are covered with gold and amalgam at various spots.

I still have my mind, though I forget things sometimes. I forgot a pair of running shorts in the shower a few weeks ago and they disappeared. I forgot a pair of dark glasses at the dining facility, but they were returned. Twice I forgot to take my ID to the dining facility. I had to walk an extra mile round trip just to eat. They won't let you in without it. I forget so much stuff that I forget what I forgot. I forget names, but that has been a chronic weakness of mine. I forget where this paragraph was going, but it had something to do with getting older.

I thought that at some time I would be old enough not to have to study to take a test. I am not there yet. I have been trying to prepare to take the Pediatric and Pediatric Heme/Onc recertifying boards when I get back. They will be closed book, computer tests, so I hope that I am still young enough to retain enough facts to pass. Learning comes slower now. This will be the first real test that I have taken in 14 years. That is pressure.

Being old here is the pits. It is not as bad as being away from your precious young children which is the case with many of the young parents here. I do miss my wife and kids and the activities they are involved in. My own kids are grown and out of the house. I really miss seeing my granddaughter as she is growing up so fast. I love the pictures which I have. I certainly am not the oldest one who is here, but there are very few older who are still in uniform.

I have had some younger soldiers come to me for advice, or just to talk a bit. At church, being the old guy kind of puts me in a leadership position and lets me have the chance to interact with the young members and hopefully influence them in a positive way. They are a fine group and I have been asked to help several times. Being able to go to church rejuvenates me somewhat each week.

Actually being "OLD" is okay, because I still actually feel and act like I am thirty. At least, I try to. My body and mind just do not cooperate frequently. My wife would say that I probably act like I am 15 rather than 51.

Hey, this would be a great place for a 12–15-year old kid. You live by an airport and planes and helicopters are coming and going all the time. They even have unmanned planes which fly by remote control. You hang out in what really is a little fort, no water, no bathroom, just your stuff, no one to tell you to make your bed or pick up after yourself. There are lots of guys around to hang out with, and not too many girls.

You get to see big trucks and heavy machinery. Things are going "boom." There is time to watch movies or play games (or study). There is time to go to the gym and build those small muscles. No one tells you when to go to bed. You can take a nap in the afternoon if you are lucky. At the dining facility (which is open even at midnight) you can eat all the food you like, about as often as you like. If you want to, you can have cake, pie or ice cream after each meal, and no one else cares. Though you can't drive, almost no one else can either, so you walk, out in the nice warm sun (that is stretching it a bit—blazing hot is the correct description).

From this old "15 year-old" guy, I wish you all the very best. I am thankful that I am still able to enjoy life and that on this birthday I can celebrate, even if it is in a different manner than usual.

Love,
Kelly

IN THE EMERGENCY DEPARTMENT

*"I thanked them for putting their lives on the line while I work
safely here in the hospital. No thanks are necessary, they reply."*

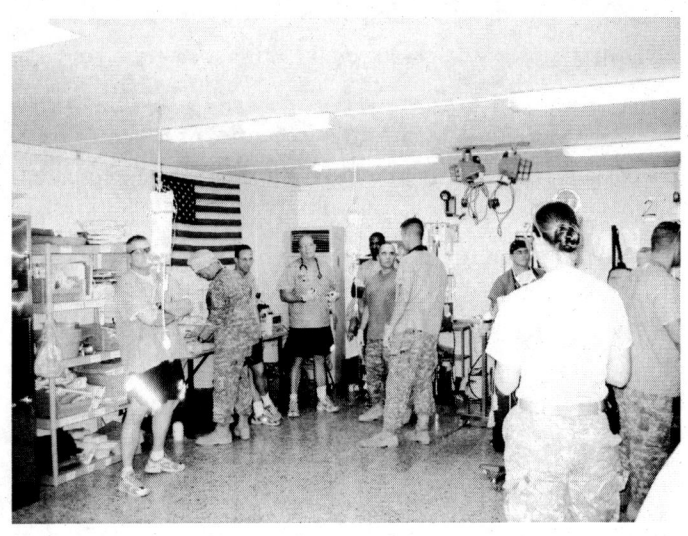

*Preparing for patients of a Mass Cal in
the Emergency Department*

16 July 2006

Dear friends and family,

Today as I was leaving the hospital there were two young men in the Emergency Department being evaluated for injuries sustained during an IED blast which hit their vehicle. Lying on a gurney, with neck collars on as a precaution, were SPC Fluty from Indiana and SPC Dane from Seattle, Washington. Their sergeant was watching over them and making sure they were okay. SGT Sutton hails from Ohio. He had a minor arm injury which he shrugged off. Their sandy tan vehicle, which is sitting outside the hospital, has "Military Police" stenciled all over it. Their unit has been here for eight months. This is the third direct hit from an IED these three soldiers have taken. Fortunately no one has been injured badly.

They, like so many, are out in the cities of Iraq on a regular basis. I talked to them a bit about that and asked if they ever give out toys, balls, etc. and they said that they do. They do what they can to spread good will, as long as they are not being shot at. They have had at least 10 near misses from IEDs. The IEDs have exploded near by, but not hit them. They have been shot at with mortars. Fortunately the mortars are not very accurate. The firing equipment is a bit primitive. It is kind of like shooting a pirate's cannon. Like horse shoes, if they are close they can count, but most of the time they do not hit their targets. If it hits you, you are in deep trouble. Lastly SGT Sutton says they take on small arms fire almost every day. At least no one is shooting at me. I thanked them for putting their lives on the line while I work safely here in the hospital. No thanks are necessary, they reply. The unit they are attached to lost a soldier last February, but fortunately none since.

I ask SGT Sutton if he would like some things to take that they could give out. He enthusiastically accepts. I have things which have been sent to me: coloring books, crayons, writing pads, a few beanie animals, and soccer balls which I have inflated. He says the soccer balls are the kid's favorite. I retrieved the items and we carried them out to his vehicle.

After we returned to the hospital, I again shook Fluty, Dane and Sutton's hands and thanked them for what they are doing here and wished them the best. They need to be careful. There is a sniper in Mosul who is on the prowl. They are very aware of this and are keeping an eye open, watching out for problems. I take some pride in good young men like these, men of different races who are a team or band of brothers. They are here trying to spread good will and provide protection, and they are getting shot at about every day. They look for explosive devices to avoid being blown up.

They are in harm's way every day. Yet, they are excited to have a few more items to take to spread the good will which our country and its people are spreading here.

These four men still have four months to go before they can return to their families. I know prayers are being offered by mothers, fathers and some family members and friends, somewhere for them. Hopefully they will make it back safely. Hopefully we all will.

ANOTHER CHILD IS INJURED

"I am very glad and thankful that Iesha will Not be among those who were killed, at least not now, and hopefully never. This country still faces a long struggle for freedom. She will have to grow up here."

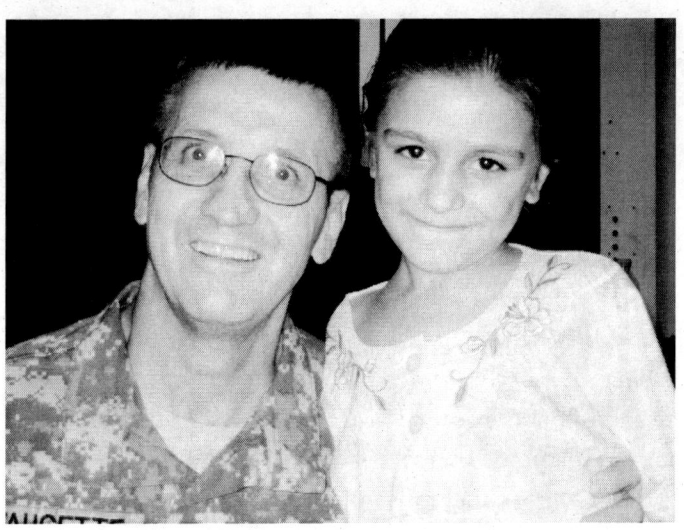

I pose with Iesha after she had recovered.

22 July 2006

Dear family and friends,

Sitting on my 'desk' in my room is Thursday's *Stars and Stripes* paper, July 20, 2006. The headline reads, "Deadly Season for Iraqis." During May and June, almost 6000 civilians in Iraq were killed, according to a U.N human rights report. On page 3 the article follows.

The paper says that according to the United Nations report, since 2003 almost 50,000 Iraqi civilians have been killed. It reports that this May and June 5,818 were killed and the number wounded is reported to be at least 5,762. I have come to know some of those who were wounded, know them well. Some are children. The numbers are up from the first part of the year.

Most of these deaths and injuries are due to insurgents killing Iraqis. Some of the insurgents are also Iraqi, and some are not, but are terrorists invading here from other countries. I heard that there was a civil war here before I came, but you didn't hear much about battles as we think of in a war. In our civil war, soldiers in different uniforms lined up and fought each other. Here, it is the civilians sneaking up, exploding bombs which are sometimes homicide bombs as they kill others and take their own lives. They are often indiscriminant, taking the elderly, women and children. Most of the casualties from bombings are innocent civilians. In this country it is hard to tell the Iraqi civilian from the war fighter.

The killings and civil war were going on for years before we came to this country. In spite of how bad it is now, it is better for most of the people than it used to be. They now have hope for peace and an end to this nonsense. Yet many are getting tired again of the ongoing fighting and with the U.S. being on their soil. They are starting to turn the blame on us.

The paper says, "Civilian casualties resulted mainly from bombings and drive-by shootings, from indiscriminate attacks, in neighborhood markets or patrol stations, or following armed clashes with the police and security forces. Civilians were also targeted or become 'unintended' victims of insurgent or military actions."

I have seen the unintended victims, but also many are the intended victims.

The paper is filled with other accounts of bombs and gunmen. "Rockets exploded Wednesday…in the green zone." "Sixteen other bodies were found in widely separate parts of the country." Unfortunately, "A 1st Armored Division soldier was killed in Iraq by roadside bomb." This morning a soldier in our hospital was given his second purple heart. On his chest is the tattoo, "lucky." Indeed he is truly very lucky to still be with us, but will be heading out of the country to Landstuhl Regional Medical Center tomorrow due to the injury. The injury was from our unfriendly sniper and our soldier was shot through the neck. The shot was a fraction of an inch away from vital structures and taking his life.

A Vehicle Bourn Improvised Explosive Devise (VBIED) or car bomb exploded at one of our gates last week. No one was hurt too badly. Mortars came in yesterday and the alarms went off, "Incoming, Incoming," and I scurried into the hospital. One of our Combat Support Hospital workers took a small piece of shrapnel to her neck. She is doing fine.

Relatively few of those killed in Iraq recently are by our troops. We are here to help keep peace at this time. Further down on the newspaper page it says we have lost 2555 members of the U.S military. At least 2,020 of these have died as the result of hostile actions, according to the military's numbers.

Our soldiers are on guard all of the time. Many face daily threats and must be aware of things out of the ordinary, like cars apparently trying to block their path and slow down their convoys and Strykers. If they are forced to slow down, a trap could be set and another IED go off. The insurgents love to film such things, and I have seen the films.

I think that the Iraqi people are caught in a dilemma and sometimes confused as well. If they are driving and the Americans come up behind them they often do not know what to do. If they speed up, they may think the Americans will think they are afraid and running and thus they think they might be shot. If they slow down the Americans may think a booby trap is coming and fire shots as warning shots to stop a potential IED getting too close to their vehicles. These soldiers and these civilians are often young men and women out to do what is right, but also fearing inside for their lives and those of their friends and brothers.

All of this really leads up to yet another pediatric patient who came in a few days ago, Iesha, who is a 6-year old girl. Iesha was sitting in the back seat of a car. The story is not 100% clear, but as best as I could tell from what was said, it happened like this. The driver, her uncle, saw a Stryker coming up behind him at a closing speed. The car in front was going slowly, so he slowed down and then moved over to get around. Apparently the Coalition forces thought they were being blocked so they fired into the car avoiding the driver. They couldn't even see the little girl sitting in the back seat. She was hit.

She cried out as she touched her back where there was blood. Somehow the cars stopped as did the Coalition forces and the injury was recognized. She had first aid administered. IVs were started and she was alert and fighting. In route the IVs came out and by the time she got to the CSH she was in deep shock. I believe that a young American Soldier was somewhat in shock as well. He did not see another choice and yet he could now tell that this turned out wrong. Her uncle stayed with her, his clothes, a long white robe, covered with her dark red blood from his chest to his feet. He had obviously held her close.

I stared an intra-osseous line (an IV into a bone) in a few seconds in a bone of her leg, and we gave her medicines which put her to sleep so she could be intubated. Fluids were started and another line was started. Blood was drawn for basic labs including a type and cross for transfusion. There was a small entrance wound and a large exit wound. On the floor below the gurney was a rapidly growing puddle of blood.

She needed to go to the operating room as soon as possible to stop the bleeding. She needed blood to save her life. The Universal donor blood was started before we knew her blood type. She was so pale. Death was creeping in upon her. One unit and then another was pushed in as she was being prepped for surgery. Her hematocrit, or blood level, came back at 13, which is exceedingly low, and that number could still have been artificially high with the ongoing blood loss. The other labs showed how bad the shock was. Her pH was very low at 6.8 due to acids building up in her body. She would die soon without help and we were fighting to keep death away.

She got another unit of blood and another and then fresh

frozen plasma to replace the depleted coagulation proteins and help stop the bleeding. Whole blood would be best as it had not only red cells, but platelets and the proteins she needed to help the surgeons get the bleeding under control. By now it was late evening and volunteer donors from the hospital rolled up their sleeves to give the life saving blood. This would be a team effort.

About ten holes were found in her bowels. They were repaired enough to stop the bleeding. A large area of muscle and flesh were gone from her side. Her pelvis was shattered and bleeding badly. Labs were being sent and acted upon. After several hours, she was finally stable. Eleven units of red cells were unthawed and given as well as seven packs of plasma and two doses of a special coagulant medicine called Activated Factor VII. Though it is very expensive and is not yet approved for bleeding due to trauma, we feel that the benefit significantly outweighs the risk. It is seen as a miracle drug which is saving lives. She also received whole freshly donated blood from six soldier donors within the hospital. She received 5–6 times her own total blood volume before the bleeding was stopped and she was stable.

Since that time, she has required more surgeries and suffered from the results of the acidosis and massive transfusions. Nevertheless, she is now doing much better and is awake and looking around. Tomorrow she will come off of the ventilator and with time she will be waving, and dancing.

I feel terrible for the soldier who may not yet know if she survived. I feel bad for her uncle, the driver who didn't know how to stay out of harm's way. I feel bad for our soldiers who are doing their best in a bad situation. I hate to judge, but hate to see people shot who should not have been. Enough have died already.

I feel bad for the many civilians who are being killed in this country, regardless of how they are killed. I am very glad and thankful that Iesha will not be among those who were killed, at least not now, and hopefully never. This country still faces a long struggle for freedom. She will have to grow up here. I hope we leave her a safe place with no guns, no bombs and no intended or unintended injuries.

THE PLANE

"When your plans are changed at the last minute it tends to make you frustrated, upset and depressed."

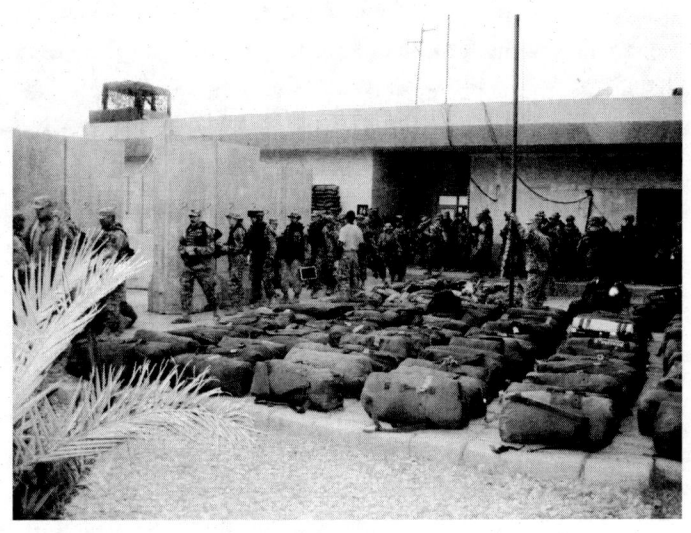

Duffle bags lay out as soldiers move

30 July 2006

Dear family and friends,

I hope all of you are doing well. I have heard some good news from the mainland. It is always good to hear that family members are doing well. I also got some news that keeps me praying for some of my cancer patients back home, as I pray for each of you. I appreciate everyone's support and friendship.

Time is marching on and another week has passed quickly. This has been both a busy week and yet an uneventful week. It has been steady, but there have been no real big events to report.

Tuesday as I walked to the MWR center to call home I noticed a big transport plane at the end of the runway. You must walk by the terminal to get to the phones. Often there are planes there, planes and helicopters of various sizes and shapes. Sometimes big birds with McChord AFB written across their tails are sitting at the end of the runway. I think on those days of hitchhiking or sneaking on as a stow-away since McCord is back in Tacoma, a few miles away from home. At a minimum I hope that my good friend, Rich Poston, who is an Air Force pilot and flies one of those, will show up to say hello, but so far he has not been able to make the trip.

Well, back to the story... A big C-17, transport plane was at the end of the runway and the loading dock in the back was down. Out of the belly of this plane was marching a whole group of new American Soldiers, all in their full battle rattle, helmets and individual body armor in place. It is an impressive sight and I wished that I had my camera to take pictures. You are not supposed to take pictures there and since I didn't have my camera with me, I couldn't follow the temptation anyway. I was in my PT uniform, T-shirt and shorts with a protective reflector belt. I must have looked rather vulnerable to them compared to their protective armor, and that feeling you have when you finally arrive in country. I am sure I was significantly cooler than they were. I remember the time when I got here. We arrived in the middle of the night, so it wasn't so impressive I am sure. You feel that you suddenly could be attacked at any time and you start looking for the enemy on all sides. The new unit is arriving from Ft. Lewis. I think to myself, perhaps I know someone getting off of the plane. In fact the next day I ran into a cardiologist who I know from Madigan, who will be stationed next door at Morez. He had come with this unit.

The next day as I was running in the morning, a big civilian plane took off and was in the air a mile down the runway near where I was running. I guessed that a group of soldiers may have been leaving as this is the type of plane they would fly in.

Two days later, early in the morning, as I was heading back from my run I saw a big group of soldiers with their bags all laid out in an open area. I had heard that a unit, the 171st from Alaska, was leaving, so I assumed it was these guys. I thought to myself, they are pretty lucky to be headed back. They have been here a year and must be excited to see their families again. It was curious to me though, for they were walking around without their battle rattle, which is the travel uniform. Just a few yards further down the road, a couple of young female soldiers were working together to carry a duffle bag, but away from the assembly area and not toward it. I wondered what was happening with them. Perhaps it was the wrong bag, too full, or some other mistake had happened.

The phones had been down the night before because of some tactical things. They were still down as far as I knew. President Bush had announced that we would be sending a bunch of new troops to Baghdad. In rounds at the hospital that morning the pieces of the puzzle came together. I learned that the 171st, which was ready to leave, had been detained. Part of the unit had left the day before and now was on hold in Kuwait. The group I had seen in the morning was picking up their bags and returning to their CHUs, or living quarters. I am sure there are some unhappy folks in that group. At the last minute their plans had been changed. It sounds like they will be here for another four months. When your plans are changed at the last minute it tends to make you frustrated, upset and depressed. They are willing to be here and most like what they are doing. A few are not happy at all on a day to day basis, but in my experience the disgruntled are the exception. I doubt that this extension was welcomed by many, if any. About everyone is ready to go home when the time comes, whether that is after a three month assignment (Air Force), six months or a year.

Friday afternoon at lunch the DFAC (Dining Facility) was fuller than I have ever seen it. You could hardly find a place to sit and eat. There certainly are more people here for the time being than there have been.

Obviously I don't know if the presidential announcement will affect the 47th CSH, my unit. Rumor is that it will not, but deep down many wonder if it might. No one really knows for sure, until they are on the plane out of the region. Until that happens, you never know. We will have to wait and see. As for me, I am still planning on being home in October. I have board exams to take and so I will be allowed to be home for them, I am pretty sure.

I think of the families back home who also got the news. My heart goes out to them as much or more than it does to the soldiers who had their bags packed to go home. Thanks to those who support us over here, to those who worry, pray and anxiously wait for our return. Thanks to those whose plans have been changed and who will stay and work and fight on in harm's way for another four months.

I hope you all have a great week. I hear it is hot there. Outside it is near 120 degrees here, so at least you can be thankful you are not here. I do appreciate air conditioning.

SPREAD OF FREEDOM

"Because of what we are doing now, the world will hopefully be safer for my grandchildren."

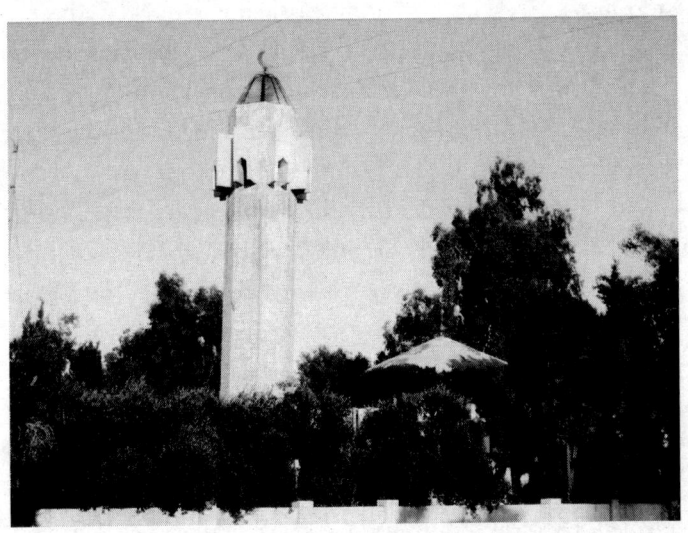

A Mosque on FOB Diamondback, Mosul

6 August 2006

Dear family and friends,

In a sense it is hard to believe that August is here. Time is passing quickly as far as getting done the things I would like to do, but is dragging as far as being away from you, my friends and family. In my experience, the longer you are in a place, the more things there are to take up your time, leaving less elective time, and that is happening even here.

We had another large mass casualty event the other night with 17 patients coming to the hospital, including two brothers, one 8 and one 15. The eight-year-old was hurt the worst of the boys and had a piece of shrapnel enter his chest and stop just a fraction away from his heart. He had to have a chest tube to evacuate the blood and air in his chest cavity. Their father was hit badly by the shrapnel and was killed. The father's body protected a three-year old brother who was safe, we found out later. The father leaves four boys and five girls to be raised by their mother with whatever help they can get. It is a tragic thing. Someone brought the IED to a soccer field where kids were playing and around ten people were killed (varying reports). It just makes no sense to me. Now this 15-year-old boy will be the man of the house. What will the future bring for this family?

Not all is work, as there was time this week to have a barbeque. Greg Lee, who has become a very good friend, headed it up and cooked up ribs, steak, and prime rib in a big smoker that looks more like a water heater from the outside. Some creative person had converted a hot water heater into a smoker, with shelves, a chimney and a place for coals. People from the hospital were invited and a good time was had by all. It even broke out into a water fight by the end, in good Faucette tradition. Our family reunions often end with water being sprayed and thrown on everyone.

We had an awards ceremony and COL James Polo, the hospital commander, gave a very interesting short talk about the region, the people, what we are doing and our own future. With some units being extended in Iraq, it has obviously been on people's minds as to whether we might be extended as well. As he looks at it, it does not appear to be in the cards to extend, giving the known going and coming units. Nevertheless, things could change, but he feels it would be very unlikely.

In this country there are not all just Iraqi people, but there are different factions, Sunni, Shiite and other religions. There are Arab and Kurdish (many who are Christian), and they do not mix well. You can not send a Kurdish person to an Arab hospital as they will fear for their life, as an example. In the US we have had our problems related to prejudice. We still perhaps have our groups to include White America, Black America, Mexican, Asian and Native Americans, etc. The difference hopefully is that we can mix and are not at war with each other any more, though there are still gangs which fight in our city streets. We can and should all be Americans together. There are not bombs going off by one group trying to kill those of another group.

The fighting here has been going on for 1500 years or more, longer than there has been an America, longer than there has been oil production, longer than people can remember. The fighting goes on and we somehow cannot stop it easily. Why does the fighting go on? Part of it is their belief in a cause that is seen as greater than now, greater than individuals, greater than families. The cause is to have Islam spread across Africa and Europe, from Spain to Iraq to Pakistan and beyond, and across the world. They want no separation of church and state and see no value in that. Someday they envision the world united under one Muslim leader. The way to make that happen is apparently to destroy anyone who is not part of that group. This goal is not a short term goal, but may take decades and if they can contribute in a small way, then they must believe that their life could be seen as a success. If they lose their own life in the cause and become a martyr, even a self-induced martyr, then they believe there is honor to that. Life here is not so good, so things must be better in the next life. They also believe in life beyond the grave.

In my own faith we are taught to share our belief. Christ did say to "Go unto all the World," teaching and converting people. There have been many who have killed in the name of God, regardless of the name given to God. How can one spread the word and not end up in the same situation as the terrorist groups who would spread their system by the sword? One of the fundamental beliefs of my church, an article of faith, says that "We claim the privilege of worshiping God according to the dictates of our own conscience and allow all men [and women] the same privilege, let them worship how, where and what they may."

The profoundness of that statement has taken on new meaning for me while being here. This statement, written in 1830, was way ahead of its time. We were ourselves persecuted, driven and threatened with extermination for our beliefs. What if all of the world would take this on, let all people worship how, where or what they may? Each could learn of each other's beliefs and each could decide. If someone wanted to become a Christian of one church or another or become a Muslim or a Buddhist, then that person could do so without fear of losing their life or job or place in society. If one wanted to covert from Islam to Christianity then they could do so. This is not allowed in Iraq, nor generally in the Muslim world. Such a change could easily result in death for the convert. True religious freedom and tolerance would mean one could openly share their beliefs. Allowing someone to choose can only happen if choice is free and available. The sword would not be the deciding factor, but one's own understanding and feelings could lead each to a decision they believe and felt was right.

Having different views and different choices is a good thing. We then live and learn. There are consequences to our choices and we learn what leads to peace and joy or to pain and anguish individually. I still think that certain values, certain choices are right and others are wrong. I think that the outcome of those choices ends up being evident. There is right and wrong. There is opposition. The difference is that the individual can choose. When wrong choices are made there are consequences and one learns not to make that wrong decision again. That leads to progress and growth.

In the end, I still believe that wrong will fail and right will prevail, and that we will have peace on earth and good will toward man. I believe that setting off a bomb and killing Iraqi police and children at the end of a soccer game is wrong. I believe that not being able to go to a hospital in Baghdad or taking your child who needs corrective heart surgery because you fear for your life, because you are Kurdish and they are Arabs, is wrong. I have been trying to get a small child who needs heart surgery to Medical City, Baghdad, but the family is afraid to go, and if we can not make something happen, then this child will likely eventually die of a problem which could be fixed. His Kurdish father is a patient in our hospital and I saw the baby when the family came to visit.

I believe that some of the people here have much to learn. Some believe the same as I do, and are willing to let me be a Christian and they can be a Muslim and say their prayers in the hospital at the appointed times as does the father of one of my patients, Iesha. He then can get up and shake my hand and be thankful for America as a great place. It isn't only America that is great, but it is our beliefs that are great. All people have certain rights, the right to life, liberty and the pursuit of happiness, the right of freedom of religion, and the right to worship God according to the dictates of our own conscience and the wisdom to let others do the same.

A pioneer is one who goes before to prepare the way. Many wonder if our military being in Iraq has or can make our own country safer from terrorists. I really doubt that we have had significantly fewer terrorist acts committed on U.S. soil in the last three years than we might have had otherwise. Nevertheless things are going on in Israel, Lebanon and across the Middle East. Terrorists desire to someday rule the world and to do so by force if necessary. I have no doubt but that the world in the future will be safer because we came here near the heart of the evil. Because of what we are doing now, the world will hopefully be safer for my grandchildren.

In medicine we try to stop disease before it is really problematic. We treat diabetes to prevent blindness, kidney failure and the loss of feet and legs down the road. We give immunizations to prevent disease. We wash our hands to stop the spread of disease. I am thankful that such things can be prevented. I am thankful that we can worship how and what we desire and that we can allow others to do the same.

Here we are protecting our country from the spread of terrorist ideas and actions by stopping them at the root. We are protecting Spain, Iraq, Europe and the world. If people can not see that then I feel they are very short sighted.

NURSES AND MEDICS

"Over the years I have seen many incredible nurses and perhaps have not told them thanks enough. I have not told them how much I admire their work, their skills and their service."

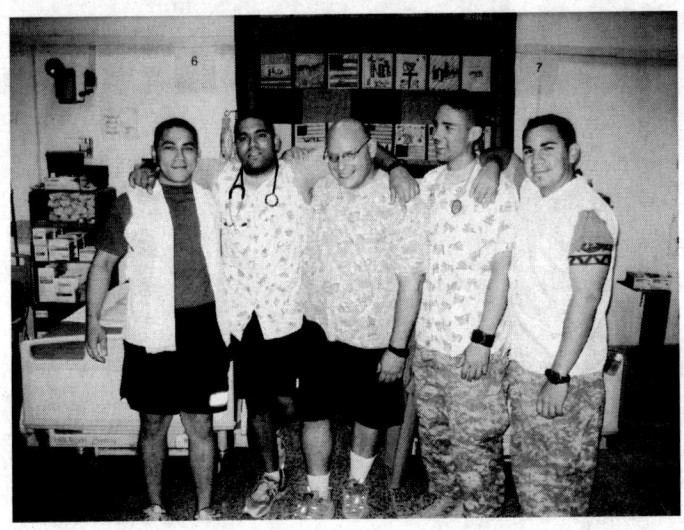

A group of our 47ᵗʰ CSH medics clown around in designer scrubs

13 Aug. 2006

Dear family and friends,

We have had a relatively quiet week at the 47th CSH, which is good for us, and more importantly good for our soldiers and for the Iraqi Police, Army and civilians. There are certainly still bad things happening in this country, but we were spared a bit. We have changed our policy and rather than keeping patients here so long, we have sent some of our patients to local hospitals. This is to be prepared for the worst case scenario as more troops are going to Baghdad.

I recently read that the Mosul Iraqi Army successfully stood up to a bunch of insurgents, where before they were unable to do so. Earlier this year they fled and now they stand strong. This is a good thing for the country.

IEDs still explode, but they do not all hit their targets. The last big blast that affected us was at a soccer stadium, as I mentioned last week. The one before that hit a bus of Iraqi police. Unlike the injuries which occurred when I first got here, we are seeing more burns. They have taken to using less shrapnel and more liquid fuel accelerant. Rocks and metal have one effect on the body, flames have another.

Burns can be devastating and hard to treat. I must say that I have learned a great deal about burn care in the last weeks. For not being a burn center, I think that we have done a great job here. We have also transferred many patients to burn centers in the country and based on a follow-up today when one of them came back, it looks like they are doing a good job. This is good as well. We have seen some patients not survive from the burns, and some who will have significant disfigurement.

It is in taking care of one of these burn patients that I got my inspiration for what I really want to say this week. We have two Iraqi men on the ward. Their faces were burnt quite badly, as were their arms and hands. They are recovering quite well actually, though both have pneumonia resulting from lung injury from the burns. They are just starting to take things by mouth, which is good. They can not eat by themselves because their hands are wrapped in big bulky dressings, so they must be fed at this time.

Most days I am able to go through the ward and hospital and give out a piece of candy, a small candy bar or other small treat which has been sent to me by good people who have offered to help. Of the treats which were sent to me is the Otter Pops or freeze pops. We have a small freezer on the ward which I use to freeze the long popsicles. I was giving one to each patient on the ward, and it was obvious that my two burned friends could not eat their frozen treat, because of their bandaged hands. Their mouths are still sore from the burning flames and I thought that this treat would be ideal for them.

I cut off the end and offered to feed the pop to them a bite at a time, pushing the frozen treat out the top as is done. They were leery at first (perhaps they never had a frozen Otter pop). After a taste they were obviously pleased, though with their facial burns they can not show full expression. I have done this for a couple of days and it is a very little thing, but so much appreciated by them. I thought of this small service, and how good it felt. I then thought of something else.

The nurses on the ward do this type of thing all day, every day. They give the little services the patients can not do for themselves, and it is not always pleasant. These burn patients must be fed if they are to take anything by mouth. The nurses feed them. They also gently wash the patient's bodies, apply the healing balms, the ointments, the dressings. They clean out wounds and gently cover them up. They clean their beds and change the soiled linens, often several times a day as many patients are not able to control their bowels and bladder.

The nurse is truly a care provider in a way that most physicians are not. The nurse spends time with the patient, minute by minute, hour by hour, day after day. As a doctor, we come in, quickly examine the patient, perhaps do a procedure and write orders for the nurses to take care of the patient, and they do it. The surgeon often saves lives by the knife and thread and needle. Their skill is incredible. The internist or pediatrician comes up with diagnoses and manages medicines, etc. But, it is the nurse who does so much of the healing.

It is true that patients often look up to the doctor, but today, as I have throughout my career, I look up to the nurses. They are incredible angels, and are skilled in their profession. The nurses do what no one else will do for the patient and for their families.

Over the years I have seen many incredible nurses and perhaps have not told them thanks enough. I have not told them how much I admire their work, their skills and their service. I can think of many times when a nurse has saved me from doom. "Dr., do you really want to order this, or could you order that?" I have seen nurses feeding little children on my pediatric floors for years. I have seen them give chemotherapy and sit and talk to a patient or family. I have seen them hold the hand of a dying child or that of a parent losing a child.

When I was student and young resident, let me assure you the nurses of the Neonatal Intensive Care Unit knew more about what was going on there than I did. I have seen them wrap a tiny infant so carefully in a blanket to let a young mother hold her tiny premature baby for the first time. Any young pediatrician would be well advised to listen to them. I can think of great nurses in the clinic, on the ward and with whom I worked from my residency to my fellowship and as a pediatric hematologist/oncologist. I must name Kim Fay and Susy Burlingame, my nurses at MAMC. They are two of the best.

Here at the 47th CSH, we have great nurses and medics, both men and women. We have corpsmen that are incredible. We have Licensed Practical Nurses, Registered Nurses, Specialists, Sergeants, Lieutenants and Captains and they are all incredible and make a great team.

It is a pleasure to work with them. I dare not begin to name names, for I would leave some out, but I am impressed by these fine young professionals. I am impressed by the medics who have an incredible role in the military as combat life savers.

To the nurses and corpsmen of the 47th CSH, to those of Madigan Army Medical Center, and of all of the hospitals and clinics where care is provided everywhere: I salute you and thank you for the great love and service that you give. I recognize your compassion and recognize the great profession of the nurse, especially the Army nurse and the medic who put their lives on the line to provide the service they give. We can not, do not, say thanks enough. Thank you!

A MULTINATIONAL FORCE

*"Education and literacy will overcome
superstition and ignorance.
These will lead to understanding and then to wisdom
and from wisdom to freedom.
Freedom will lead to hope and prosperity."*

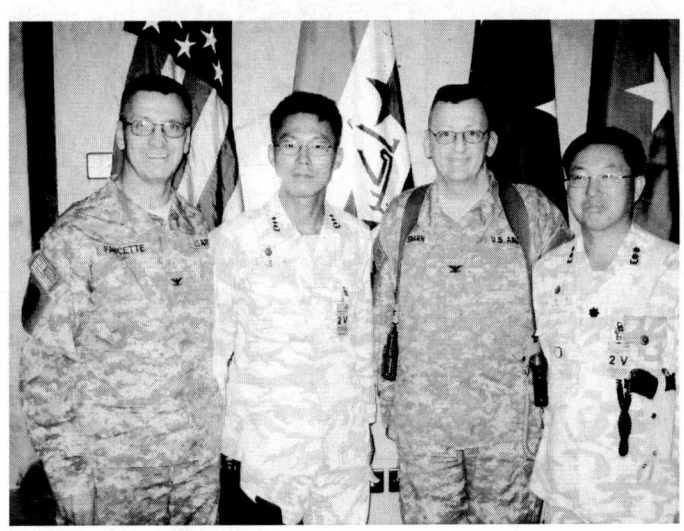

Myself, The Korean leaders and COL Steven Swan

15 Aug. 2006

Dear family and friends,

Tonight as I jogged home from the gym a tune kept going through my head, as it often does when I jog. This tune is one that I have not thought about for a very long time, but I do know where the key word came from. That key word is friends.

I grew up outside of Sanford, Colorado, a town of about 800 people. The people in that area were farmers, for the most part, but we had our cowmen (real cowboys with cows they herded on horses and the whole bit). They still are farmers and cowboys there and the song in my mind involved them.

The tune comes from the musical "Oklahoma," "The Farmer and the Cowman Should be Friends." The farmer and cowman in Oklahoma, and in my home town, sometimes had their problems. A cow would get into some farmers field and it wasn't good for the farmer's field, or sometimes for the cow if the wrong crop were growing. All in all they got along and were friends.

So today that little tune is going through my mind and I think of our country and of Iraq. In our country we have made great strides to get along, to work together or side by side regardless of differences in ethnic origin, color, religion or gender. I think that is especially true in the military, where we work as a team and for the most part do not really pay attention to such items. Each person can be respected for what they do, and how well they do their job. We as Americans still have work to do, but I think we have made great strides.

In Iraq there is still much tension. Individual groups and leaders have their own militias and there is fighting, but this week I got to see a different side of the country where they are making great strides. Much of their success comes because of the work of the multinational force that is here in this country. They are truly helping.

Though the United States is here with by far the largest numbers and we have the most dangerous mission, let me assure you that we are not alone in the work of Iraq. Around us on this FOB we are guarded by the Albanians. When I run by the perimeter of the base in the morning I holler, "good morning" to the Albanians as they stand guard from their towers and they always greet me back, "hello." They are good friends.

Much of the work is being done by a large group from Turkey. One of their men was hit by a mortar and was injured badly. He was brought to our hospital where he was cared for until he unfortunately died from his injuries. The Turkish workers were so appreciative of the work that we did that they invited us to their dining facility for a splendidly prepared dinner. This was one of the best meals we have had since being here. They extended the invitation for us to come back any time and eat there, and we have taken the opportunity to get some of their wonderful fresh baked bread a couple of times. Let me assure you I would get bread more often if they were closer.

There are workers on the FOB from the Philippines, Nepal, Italy, and I believe many countries around the world. There are many Iraqi nationals who risk their lives by coming to work here each day and are friends of the United States. Their wishes for their country are the same as we have for ours: safety, security, freedom and prosperity.

In the south of the country a large group of English

Soldiers controls the area including the main road and supply route to Baghdad. With the increased activity in the center of the country they are worried about security and safety in that region, but they stay on and continue to be our friends.

This week COL Steven Swan, commander of the 30th Medical Battalion, came to visit us. He gave us a report of things happening elsewhere in the country. He and a group of people from our FOB went to Irbil, Iraq, where 3000 Korean soldiers are stationed. Though I did not get to go, I learned much from those who did and from the pictures and stories they brought back. LTC Greg Lee M.D. from Tripler Army Medical Center, Hawaii, was full of enthusiasm as he showed us the many pictures of his visit and a video he received. He stated, "This is what we should be doing."

The Koreans came to Iraq and set up a base they called "Zaytun," which means "olive branch," a symbol of peace. They came and moved into a desert spot and began to build. At first the Kurdish people, who live there, were leery. There was fighting going on and mortars dropped in on them as they built. With time they began to have an impact on the people and the Kurds began to trust them, and helped to oust any potential insurgents. For over a year the area has been secure and there are no more mortars falling.

There are paintings and signs saying, "Koreans and Kurdish are Friends." The Koreans have focused on the hearts and minds of these good people. They began to help them recover from the effects of war in their area over the last 40 years. They have built homes, businesses, schools, parks and friendships. They have sent some Kurdish Iraqi leaders to Korea for training and to witness the strength and progress of Korea. These people will bring back ideas and wisdom for Iraq. The Koreans have built a vocational school and are educating and graduating Kurdish workers in skills such as computers, automobile mechanics, diesel engines and generators, operating heavy equipment and cooking or baking. The computer course is especially popular and fills up quickly. The Kurds can now go out with their skills and build their own country.

The Koreans have a hospital and they treat the Kurdish people. They give women and children care. They do long-needed surgeries. They give hope and comfort. We on the other hand take care of the wounded and broken, those hit by bombs and bullets. It makes you wonder if we could do more. Sometimes we try, but that is not yet our mission.

The Koreans have helped drill deep wells and brought life giving water to the people. They have built a high storage tank from which water flows to homes and thirsty mouths. They have used technology to begin to build a city that did not have the resources.

The Korean/Kurdish friendship extends to sporting events, to singing and dancing together and to learning. Dr. Lee is of Korean ancestry. He was amazed as he saw Kurdish boys and girls lined up to sing the "head, shoulders, knees and toes" song, but to his surprise, they were singing in Korean. The kids were dressed in delightful colorful costumes and danced and had faces painted with little colorful decorations and balloons celebrating the honored American guests.

Education was happening for the Kurdish also in the Kurdish language. Men and women are learning to read and write. Education and literacy will overcome superstition and ignorance. These will lead to understanding and then to wisdom and from wisdom to freedom. Freedom will lead to hope and prosperity.

"Yes the farmer and the cowboy should be friends. So should the Kurds and the Arabs, the Shiites and Sunni, the people of Irbil and Mosul and Baghdad and all of the cities of Iraq."

In Irbil the people are open and teachable. They are ahead of most of the country of Iraq. There are many Christians who live and worship there. There are Moslems who live and worship there. They worship on their holy days, and then they work together the rest of the week. They have a common goal of building their community. They understand freedom and understand individual rights. They are friends. The Koreans and Kurdish are new friends. The Koreans and Americans are friends and the Kurdish and Americans are friends.

COL Swan praised the Korean leaders for their civil work. They replied that they had learned it from the Americans over the last 50 years. You see, it was not long ago that we fought a war on their soil. Theirs was a devastated and backward land where in 1964 the average salary was $100 a year. There was poverty and illiteracy, pollution and sickness. Now through our friendship, they are strong, modern and prospering. They have freedoms there. They have hosted the Olympics and are world class competitors. They are producers and builders. Each can become what they want to be, worship how they want to worship and together be friends. The Han River in Korea was formerly a dirty, polluted and dead river. It has been cleaned up and become a center of beauty and life. Along its banks are beautiful modern cities.

In Iraq there are two great rivers, the Tigris and Euphrates. They too could become the life blood of this country as they had been in the past, if the people could just learn to be friends. Who can teach them to do this? I would like to say the Americans, but I must say it is not only the Americans; it is the Koreans, Turkish, English, the Albanians and others with the Americans together, as we join hands and hearts and act as friends, a multinational peace-building team. We are here to build this nation and people, and I am thankful that I got to see what is being done by others of our team.

Yes the farmer and the cowboy should be friends. So should the Kurds and the Arabs, the Shiites and Sunni, the people of Irbil and Mosul and Baghdad and all of the cities of Iraq. The Christian and the Moslem should be friends. Perhaps someday it will be so.

REAL WAR

Nevertheless, there are problems of a huge portion here. This week I have learned that there are truly issues which will take time to fix.

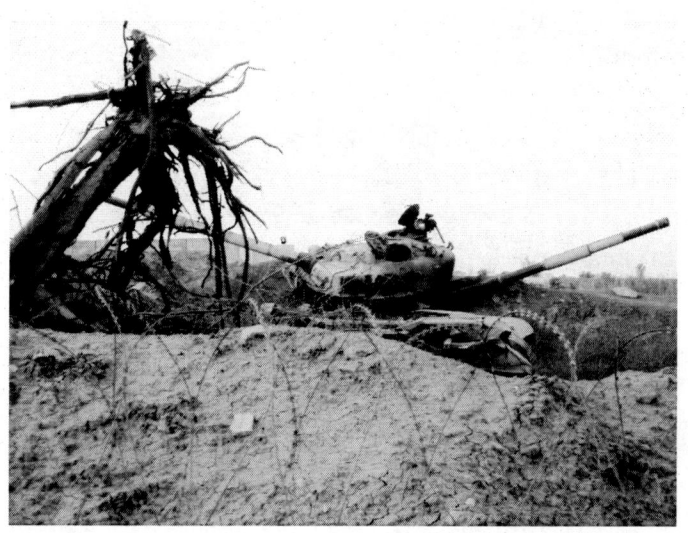

A scene from near camp Slayer in Baghdad

27 Aug 2006

Dear family and friends,

Today is my granddaughter's first birthday. I miss being with her, and with my daughter and wife to celebrate. Things are going well for me individually here. It is hard to believe that it is almost September.

Last week I wrote of how progress was being made in the Kurdish portion of Iraq where the Koreans are stationed. I also mentioned that we were a long way away from that kind of peace in Mosul and most of Iraq. This week's note is a bit less optimistic. There is still war going on here and in much of Iraq.

I spent lunch with two men who are working with the Iraqi police in Mosul. They are over the training of police in Mosul and are retired police officers from the United States. One is from Colorado where I grew up. They are pleased with some of the progress the Iraqis are making. The Iraqi police stood up to the insurgents a few weeks ago and it surprised the insurgents who were sure that they would be successful. Before the attack, the insurgents prepared and filmed public boasts for broadcasting after the attack, saying that they "had killed" several civil leaders in their attacks. The battle turned out differently than they anticipated. After the battle those same civil leaders were on TV telling of a different victory, one for Iraq, and they were very much alive.

Nevertheless, there are problems of a huge portion here. This week I have learned that there are truly issues which will take time to fix. When an insurgent is picked up as a suspect in certain crimes, such as an explosion, in Mosul the Iraqi judge must go out to investigate or there can be no convictions. The judges are afraid to go, afraid to investigate, afraid to convict. The men are therefore held for only a specified time and are then released.

In the last year I was told, there have been no real convictions. The Mosul jails are full of hundreds of insurgents and each day about 30 are released back on the streets. In another location I learned that one prison facility has about 8000 prisoners. That by itself is a good size city, whose doors are turning. We are not fighting just a few troublemakers.

Sunday, 20 Aug was my dad's 89th birthday and I could not call him for the phones were down. While the phones are generally available for part of most days, on a regular basis they do not work and no outside call can be made. Earlier in the day another one of our soldiers had been hit by a sniper through the shoulder. Miraculously he survived with no life-threatening injury. Perhaps that same sniper knew he missed, for one hour later we had another call. Another young American, a husband and father from Ft. Lewis, was hit in the back of his head. We worked to revive him and he had a strong heart, but the brain injury won in the end and he died. It was the first loss for the new Stryker unit here from Ft. Lewis. It was devastating to us all.

Monday I watched as his unit held a ceremony for him and his body was loaded into a huge transport airplane. It was a sobering and an impressive event. The bagpipes played "Lament." The unit marched and saluted. The greatest of respect is shown in ceremony and in our hearts. The men often gather together and pray after this. The end of this ceremony was disrupted by the warning signals of "incoming" and a call to the "bunkers." We took cover, but did not hear any explosions and soon the all clear was given.

There have been several Americans killed by snipers since I have been here. About every 8 days one seemed to hit. Before I arrived a man had been picked up who said he worked every 8 days, got a week off and then worked again. Interrogators said he was a sniper, but there was no real evidence, so he was released, and then the regular killings began. A few of our men were hit on the 8th day and were injured but lived. This was again true on last Sunday, but hopefully the pattern will finally end.

Good news came Sunday night that the Iraqi police caught a suspected sniper, with a car full of high powered weapons and gun powder on his hands. I hope they got him, but do 'they' have enough evidence to keep him and stop the killings? How long might he be detained until he is let go? Some worry that if he only shoots Americans he will not be seen as a threat to the Iraqis, so he may be released rather quickly.

In the hospital we had a man who blew off his own leg several weeks ago making an IED. His partner was killed in the same blast. He survived 18 hours before being brought in with gangrene in his stump. We fixed him. He was classified as an "Anti-Iraqi Army" (AIA) on our census board (the politically correct name for a terrorist). At least for a time, then he was somehow taken off of the terrorist list because of an evidence problem. Another of our patients, who was on the ward with his face wired together, said of Stinky Stump, as we called him, "He is the man who shot me." This man had his mandible shattered and his life nearly taken. He was noticeably afraid. Stinky Stump was no longer a "terrorist." Soon he got well enough to transfer to an Iraqi hospital. This terrorist was afraid to go, perhaps for his own safety. I made it clear in my discharge summary how he had been injured in the first place, while making IEDs. I don't know what happened to him.

Patients are sometimes reclassified and today one of our patients was reclassified as an AIA. Another high powered Mosul leader was brought in after being injured. We are not sure of how this happened but because of political issues he was transferred from the Iraqi system to ours, which is unusual. My two friends from the lunch room know him. They say that he is working both sides of the system. Perhaps he should be AIA as well. They say that many, perhaps 20% or more of the Iraqi police are corrupt. They are giving information to the terrorists and helping the police. Our police trainers think that many are forced to do so, or to be killed and have their families killed. It is blackmail and these people are caught in the middle, and are trying to survive.

These American police officers have been on the streets for over 2 years. They have seen lots of blasts and badness. IEDs have hit near them. They come up to a check point which is supposed to be guarded by the Iraqi Army and find that no one is around, and then an IED goes off. I was told two stories by one of our civilian police officers who trained the Iraqi police and worked with them. In the first he was with a convoy of Americans and Iraqi. The Iraqis were leading the way, and they stopped to investigate some strewn wire alongside the road. The rest of the convoy, the Americans, went on by them, only to be hit by an IED a few hundred yards further down the road. In another convoy the Iraqi were taking up the tail, when they suddenly stopped as the convoy was approaching a corner. The convoy slowed, turned the corner and was then hit by an IED. Why did the Iraqi stop? It does make one wonder whose side one is on.

Tonight I read an article from *Newsweek*, 24 July about the War in the Middle East. It says that Iran has agents which have infiltrated the Iraqi militias, the political parties and the security services. We believe that many of the terrorists also come from Syria. One man was picked up, an AIA, who had $40,000 American money on him here in Mosul this week. Where does the money come from? The article says that Iran is financing much of what happens here. Hezbollah of Lebanon, Hamas, etc. are supporting the terror.

Hezbollah was created by Iran. It is a Shiite Lebanese militia and means the "Party of God." The article says, "With Saddam's fall, free traffic is allowed in Iraq from Iran and Iraqi Shiite mullahs return from exile in Iran with Islamist messages."

This is more than a battle for freedom and against terrorists. It is in a real way another war of ideals. Religion is center. Hezbollah was able to unite two groups of serious religious difference, the Palestinian Sunni and Shiite strains of Islam, when the Palestinians were exiled from Israel and Lebanon. Those same groups are killing each other in Iraq. Hezbollah and the terrorists' ultimate goals are to unite and also destroy the infidels, which are us, as well as the Kurds, or anyone who does not follow their religion.

Let there be no doubt there is a war going on here. Mortars fly in and threaten us, though not as often as they used to. We have been in the bunkers a few times lately. It is not a good feeling. We have seen flashes of light in the middle of the night hit the airfield near us and have felt the ground shake and heard the explosions. Yes, there is war going on around us.

THE MISSIVE

A LETTER TO HER SON, BY DR. ROCHELLE WASSERMAN

Well, there is the principle that we are all human beings and that life is inherently precious; I am sure you have been learning this in Hebrew school.

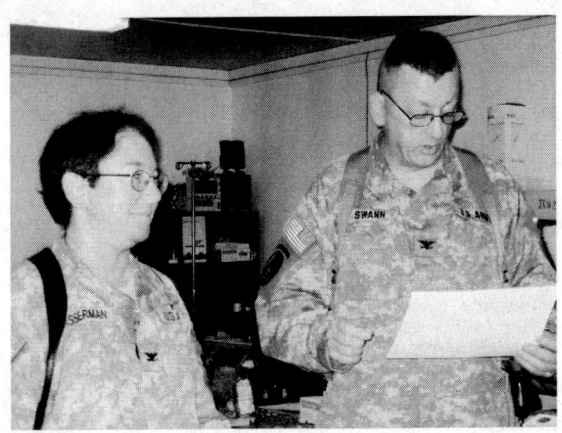

COL Rochelle Wasserman receives an award from COL Steven Swan, commander of the 30th Medical Brigade

Dr. Wasserman became a friend of mine as we worked together at the hospital. She is a family practitioner. She shared the following letter with me and agreed to let me publish it with my own should I be able to publish them. I think that it is excellent and portrays much of what we experienced, as well as gives some good advice to our American youth. I am thankful for her wisdom.

Dear Matthew,

You know I sent a long email to your younger brother Arnold and I have no intention of forgetting about you. Poppa says you have been preparing for your Bar Mitzvah, an event that will symbolically mark your passage into manhood. It seems like yesterday you were small enough to hold with one arm, but you are now 13 and almost tall enough to "eat soup off of my head." As your mom, I wish to send along my love and some words of guidance and possibly wisdom, as you prepare to assume your new status. I know studying Hebrew and Torah passages are not your favorite things to do (and probably not the favorite activities of many of your peers either) and when I was your age I too spent long hours studying arcane traditions. So I can sympathize that playing video games and hanging out with your friends after public school seems a lot more fun. I'm guessing that right now you are more enthusiastically looking forward to the party, after the service, with its food and gifts. But ultimately, what is more important than the Bar Mitzvah itself is the point of the ritual, which is to celebrate you becoming a young adult and with that, entering into the larger realm of congregation and community with its attendant obligations, privileges and satisfactions. One hopes that the new Bar Mitzvah will help make one a better Jew for having gone through extensive study of the ancient traditions and history, pondered the relationship of God to human, human to God, and human to human, and given thought on the meaning of "growing up." One hopes that they will also be better persons for the experience. I have the same expectations of you.

Because you are an "Army Brat," the war on terrorism has had a much more personal impact on you than on the vast majority of your Hebrew school classmates. Even if you were not being guided toward adulthood by nature, parents, teachers, and religious teachings, you are being unavoidably pushed by current events to leave your childhood behind faster than the norm and to become involved in adult concerns relating to this troubled world. I recall you asking, "Mom, why do you have to go? Why can't someone else do it?" I also remember you wanting to know why the US just didn't drop the Bomb and nuke Iraq into a glowing plain of glass so that the terrorists would be dead, the war over, and I wouldn't have to leave home. When you said that once I got to Iraq, that as a Colonel, I should insist on getting an office without a view, I was touched by your concern for my safety and impressed by your intelligent practical bent of mind.

I want to let you know that not only I, but the majority of the soldiers that work at the hospital have offices without views, and those that do have views of sandbags or concrete blast walls. Not pretty in the conventional sense, but to me, gorgeous given the circumstances. I know that you and the family and lots of other people worry about me being in a war zone. So far, those of us within the FOB have only been subjected to a few ineffective attacks. Earlier this year, at the height of counterinsurgency operations in Mosul, before Coalition, Iraqi Army and Police, and Peshmerga forces defeated a major insurgent attempt to completely control the city, there were more attacks, yet none of the hospital folks were killed by attacks on this base and only one person was shot and fortunately not seriously hurt. While this is not completely reassuring, statistically speaking, you can bet the savings account and your Play-Station that I will be coming home hale and hearty with nothing worse than some unpleasant memories and more war stories to bore you with. Even the infantry guys, who have it much worse than us, have a better than 95% chance of coming back alive and well.

Should the worse happen to me anyway, remember this: Things that Americans take for granted as their birth right, freedom of conscience and thought, respect for the dignity of human life, respect for property, the rule of law and the simple expectation of safety, security and goodwill between neighbors, are held in contempt by the terrorists that we are fighting today in Iraq and elsewhere who regard fairness, compromise and reason as weakness and an invitation to further mayhem and oppression. Because of this, if those ideals that Americans hold dear are to be preserved, they must for now, unfortunately, be purchased with the treasure of the taxpayers and at times the blood of patriots. It's a price I'm willing to pay to give you and other kids a chance at a better world.

You asked why I had to deploy to Iraq, the short answer is that if I wish to collect a paycheck and not be the infirmary doc at Ft. Leavenworth, I am legally obligated to follow orders. The longer answer, Matthew, is I strongly believe that if good people do nothing, evil prevails by default. I believe that what I am doing as a member of America's military is serving the cause of good at home and abroad. I am sure you have learned in both public and Hebrew school about the Holocaust and how the democratic nations ignored the plight of the Jews under the Nazis with disastrous results to not only the Jews but to the world at large. The events of 9/11 demonstrate that there are those out there that would do to Americans (and any one else they hate) what the Nazis tried to do the Jews, and they share with the Nazis and the bigoted fanatics before them, a desire to eliminate the Jews. Your Uncle Isaac, who managed to survive Auschwitz and has numbers tattooed into his arm as a grim reminder of that horrific experience, did not have the chance to directly fight against his enemies, I do.

Your question, "Why not just nuke Iraq?" is a very good one. Why not use every method at a nation's disposal to win a war? It is a question that has been debated for moral and practical reasons throughout time. The Bible records some early attempts to limit the destructive aspects of warfare to include prohibitions against willfully destroying the orchards or poisoning wells of the Israelites' enemies and requiring that Israelite warriors who wished to take to wife their female captives to have a one month period for the women to grieve for the loss of their families and were to avoid having intimate relations during this time. If at the end of that time they still wished to marry the woman, they had to treat her with respect as if she was an Israelite. If not, she was to be allowed to leave a free woman. Not only the moral thing to do, but practical, as a woman who was forced to be an Israelite was probably unlikely to raise the children along Israelite ways and it made it more likely that her husband could get a good night's sleep.

In modern times, the Geneva Convention has been the major guide on codifying what may be legitimately done to win a war, while reducing unnecessary suffering of both civilians and military personnel. But once again, why worry about, "legitimacy" or the suffering of enemy populations?

Well there is the principle that we are all human beings and that life is inherently precious; I am sure you have been learning this in Hebrew school. Based on that, even in war, a moral military is obliged to limit taking of life to what is necessary to achieve military goals and not to destroy lives without discrimination between those who are fighters and those who just happen to living in the area. Life is not a HALO 2 video game. There are no pause or replay buttons in war and real people scream and bleed and die when hurt by the violence. As a parent, I would be devastated if you were killed due to being caught in crossfire between police going after criminals, but I could accept that accidental collateral damage happens; I would be venomously vengeful if that happened deliberately. Other parents in other nations feel the same way.

A little restraint is not only the compassionate thing to do, it reduces the likelihood of making implacably hostile enemies. And that brings up an important point, that short of committing genocide, which is something loathsome to Americans, no matter how quickly a foe is defeated by military force, in the long run, if one wants to live in a freer, safer, and more prosperous world, some kind of just and lasting peace must be made. While there are no guarantees that your opponent will respond to compassion and reason, prosecuting a war without moral restraint is a sure fire way to guarantee the opposite. Much to America's credit, we have often extended a helping hand to defeated foes and in the process gained long term allies, or at any rate business partners unlikely to attack us for revenge. Even if it takes 10 or 20 years, I hope that the same will happen here, and in a small way I see it happening now even given my limited perspective from the "purdah" of FOB Diamondback, Iraq.

I realize that this missive is not typical of most Bar Mitzvah words of parental pride and advice, but your situation is anything but typical. I hope they will inspire you to be compassionate to others, proud of your heritage, and resolute in fulfilling your duties. Whether you follow me in pursuing a military career or find your destiny on another path, I hope you will be drawn to playing your part in Tikkun Olam, the healing of the world.

Love,
Mom

ALL IN THE FAMILY

My sacrifice is really nothing at all. I must count my blessings. What I can get from my time away, is perhaps more than I can give. I have learned a great deal. I have experienced a great deal.

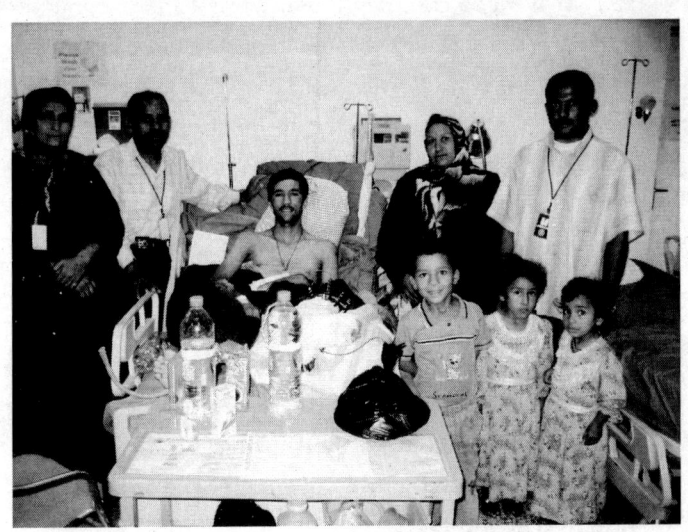

An Iraqi family gather around a wounded soldier.

3 Sept. 2006

Dear family and friends,

I hope that each of you is doing well. I wish to thank each of you for your support and prayers. Let me assure you that I feel the strength of your prayers. Thank you for your notes and for your thoughts.

I am doing well and now have arrived at a time when things are starting to wind down. That is a good feeling. I can start thinking about "next month" and being home to see family and many of you again.

I had intended on writing about another great thing that is happening in Iraq, but will save that for next week, or another time. There is a great amount of building happening here.

Today I want to comment about family and the importance of family, and things that are happening in my family. I want to recognize the sacrifices of families in our country.

When one is deployed they continue to live, pass time, work and enjoy life, or suffer if their attitudes are not good. We have good food but we are aware that there are many children and families in the world who go without. Many people get by with minimal food, and often it is hardly edible. We have places to sleep and there are many in this region who have left their homes for fear. There are many in Afghanistan and places around the world that are displaced by war, drought, floods, and by tsunamis, etc. They live in make-shift tents or out in the open with little or no shelter. We have it very good really.

There are those soldiers here who have it worse than I do, but overall we try to take care of our soldiers no matter where they are or what they are doing. The cost of protecting the American soldier in Iraq is expensive. There is body armor, fortified vehicles, air superiority, cement walls, guards, advance technology, etc. We consider it to be worth the cost for we see their lives as very precious.

The one thing that those who deploy sacrifice is being with their families. Some are gone for over a year. Some are now gone for the second or third time. Some are gone from home for the first time in their lives. Some leave little children or new wives or husbands. Some go because they are told and some go because they want to. In the end, all who are here are here based on decisions and choices they made at some time in their lives. That is the freedom we are promoting.

Being gone from family is a sacrifice that we give to make the world a better place. Being away is not fun and can make one "home sick." Being away we miss important events: births, birthdays, anniversaries, graduations, weddings and sometimes funerals. We worry from afar, we celebrate from afar, we support from afar, and we are supported from afar.

Being away, being here, is a sacrifice that we can give. A sacrifice is something that one gives for a greater cause. A sacrifice is when one goes without, in order to let someone else have the same. It might be a donation to the poor. It might be time at the bedside of a sick patient or friend. It might be working in a country across the world. Sacrifice is a good thing for the giver as well, as it builds them and helps them to be less selfish, less materialistic, and more empathetic and caring.

This week I had one niece admitted to an ICU in Georgia after being in a terrible accident. Her truck rolled several times as it left the freeway at a high speed. Her 18-month son was strapped in at her side. He was protected as the car seat held fast and the cab was not crushed down on him, but he was in a small bubble, protected by a guardian angel perhaps. There is little other explanation. He survived with some bruises and only one leg was broken.

My niece on the other hand suffered bleeding into her head. She was severely injured. There were suspected injuries to her abdomen. The physicians were not sure if she might not lose her hand as the skin was pulled off as if a glove was removed. She was placed on a ventilator and prayers were offered. She was given a blessing and more prayers were offered with fasting. She is going to make it. She will keep her hand. She is improving, but we are still waiting to see how bad the head injuries are going to affect her. We recognize our Father in Heaven, and give thanks for this miracle.

Another niece was married in Albuquerque. She was surrounded by family, including my wife and daughter. Many of my brothers and sister were there. There were smiles and a few tears and prayers offered as well. She is starting a new life with a man she loves.

The family had a reception for her and large crowds attended. The biggest supporters were family; grandparents, parents, aunts, uncles, cousins, brothers and sisters. There was one uncle missing though, one who would have liked to have been there.

Last week my granddaughter turned one. This week the family is gathered together for another wedding in Denver and I am not there. I join with my friends here, who miss being home. It doesn't matter if you are gone for the first time, if you are a newlywed, a young parent, or a grandparent; family is the one thing that you miss while you are here.

I know that there are soldiers here whose families are having troubles. All will not be better for every soldier when they return home. For some there will be difficult times, flashbacks, post traumatic stress, anger and broken families. I wish for all soldiers that returning home and to their former life will be good. When a sacrifice is offered, there are usually blessings which come and perhaps by our being away, we will return with a determination to make our families stronger, to be better sons and daughters, better husbands and wives, better fathers and mothers.

Today at church in Mosul, a brother told of the sacrifices he learned of as he talked to Iraqi soldiers and people. One thing that we have seen here is that the sacrifice we give is very little compared to that given by most of the Iraqi people. As I have said before, there are few families in this country who have not lost someone in the past 30 years. Families have been gathered up and executed in open fields. Parents have seen their children killed. Children have lost parents. Wives have seen their husbands taken or killed. Gunfire and explosions are a way of life. Many thousands have been driven from their homes with virtually nothing. Many do not have adequate food or clean water, but most still have hope for a better country, where they can be safe and have freedom. Those who have lost hope join the other side and the war continues on.

Our own sacrifice of American life must be mentioned. As of Thursday 2,096 U.S. citizens have died as a result of hostile action in Iraq. Others have been killed in accidents. A total of 2,642 members of the U.S. military will not again see their families, will not join in a welcome home, and will not hold their loved ones again. They have given the ultimate sacrifice. Others from other coalition countries have also given their all. Each has given their life for the hope of a better world for our families, our children and those of the people of Iraq. They have sealed the importance of the hope we bring with their blood.

No, I guess my sacrifice is really nothing at all. I must count my blessings. What I can get from my time away, is perhaps more than I can give. I have learned a great deal. I have experienced a great deal. That is not really a comparable sacrifice.

I thank the families who send part of themselves into harm's way, including especially my own. I would like to thank those families who have lost a vital part of their very identity, a son, a daughter, a husband or a father. I would like to thank them for their truly tremendous sacrifice. There is no way to repay them, nor to adequately recognize the sacrifice they have given.

TRIP TO BAGHDAD

I have hope that someday this might be a place where someone would want to come and visit, and could come and feel safe and secure.

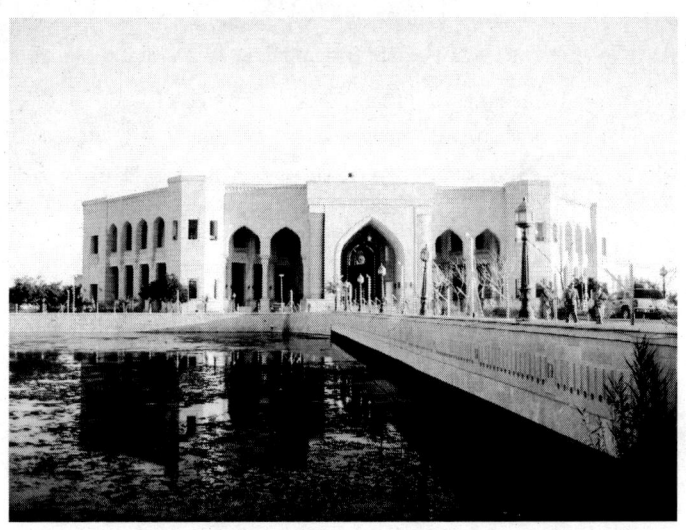

The Al-Faw Palace in Baghdad. Most Iraqi people did not know of this great complex until Saddam placed civilians in and around it as human shields when the bombing started.

11 Sept. 2006

Dear family and friends,

It has been 5 years today since America was attacked. I remember the day well. Our vulnerability was made blatantly obvious. Much has happened in those five years. Some of it is good, some not so good, and some is much debated.

I was invited to attend the "Surgeon's Conference" where the 30th Medical Brigade presented their "lessons learned" to the incoming commander. The meeting was held in Baghdad so that I got to leave FOB Diamondback in Mosul for a trip, and I am sitting in Baghdad at the JVB five-star hotel near the Al-Faw palace built by Saddam Hussein. The hotel is an impressive building. The palace is a very impressive building. As I look around at the splendor here, I wonder what this place was like five years ago. I have some idea, I think. In my mind I see very proud and wealthy groups living the good life, spending money on ornate things while around them are the very poor who can barely etch out a living.

The clerk at the hotel desk is Military and the price is good, at least for me. It is free. In my room are 10 bunk-beds. I have the top bunk by the far right corner window. Well, what do you expect for free?

I have got to see many of the buildings here on FOB Liberty. They built palaces around man made lakes, which were dug out and filled with water. I ran this morning before the sun was up to Camp Slayer where I saw the bombed out pleasure palace of Uday, who was one of Saddam's sons. I also saw the large palace called, "Victory over America." It needs some work. The name doesn't really fit for the victory never happened. This palace is now being used as barracks for the enlisted soldiers. That is Victory for America. It was still in the process of being built. Fortunately there never was a "Victory over America" and hopefully there never will be. It is good to remember that their definition of victory might well be different than ours.

It is sad to see the damage inflicted due to the fighting, but on the other hand most is preserved. In another part of the country a "captured" palace was turned over to the Iraqi people and within two weeks it was completely looted and destroyed. A beautiful building was destroyed as these would likely be if we turned them over to the people. Perhaps this is because they represent an ugly part of history. High Iraqi officials are glad that we occupy these buildings now, as we are using them and not destroying them. One thing is for sure, I have never seen a fancier gym than I saw in Camp Slayer, with marble walls and floors. I took a lot of pictures of the palaces and area this morning.

At the Surgeon's Conference I found that we have learned some important lessons in the last year and that the mission is changing. It was an impressive group of people. In the room were the two leaders of medicine in Iraq, including their surgeon general. One of them was a dentist. I got to meet them and talk with them individually for a very long time. Fortunately they speak English. They are good men who want the best for their country and its medical system.

I also got to meet and talk to leaders of other coalition medical groups to include the leader from Korea, England and Poland. They are all good men who are doing their best to provide for their troops and to help build the country. I had an especially long talk with the good physician from

Poland. He is here for his second tour. He spent two years here the first time. He has some of the same concerns I have, concerns that this country will not change significantly until the people have individual freedoms.

There is good and bad news, as is often the case in Iraq. The number of medical schools has increased from seven to sixteen. The number of graduates is increasing. They are well trained, but many of them are leaving the country. There have been 157 physicians killed in the last few years. Physicians are high targets for kidnapping and for terrorists, as are other educated professionals. People feel they have money, and they do have importance and prestige. If you take away the community physician, you demoralize the community.

In the same way, if we are unable to provide good medical care for the soldiers, they would be less willing to fight. It is important that they can feel they will be taken care of if they are hurt. The same goes for the Iraqi Army and the Iraqi police.

Right now with all the factions and local militias in Iraq, their Army is about the only group which is united and covers boundaries of religion, location, tribes, and local leadership. If this country is to succeed, it is important for them to be able to take the leadership role, and to protect the government until it can establish credibility.

The Korean group has done a great job in not only helping take care of the Iraqi people and their medical needs, but to begin to build and educate the people. Their area in the North where the Kurdish live is generally considered secure. Their leader is a man of wisdom and has good foresight. He gave a good overview of the lessons they have learned. His English is as good as my Army talk. I missed about 10% of what was said by some presenters in the conference, due to all the acronyms.

Our mission has been different, and part of what needs to happen now is to let the Iraqi medical system work. In Mosul just a year ago they were able to take care of about 40% of their emergencies, and now they are taking care of more than 80%. That explains why we have been less busy with trauma recently.

The system is working better in Baghdad as well, though the 10th Combat Support Hospital located here remains very busy. Things have to be busy as there were over 1,500 violent deaths of Iraqi citizens in Baghdad in August. That means a lot are also injured. The number is about the same as in July, I read today. It seems that the number for May and June was about 1000 a month, but I do not recall for sure.

Our mission here is to somehow help the Iraqi Army stand up, and they need to know that they have medical care. Plans for a military hospital to be built in Baghdad are in place and before 6 months are up, it should be built. Unfortunately for now, they have no specific plans for staffing it, but if you build it, they will come. Perhaps some of those newly trained Iraqi physicians will stay here and perhaps some who left will come back.

Their Surgeon General told me that one thing they desperately need is nursing personnel. There is a big shortage of them. We are having some of the same shortage in the U.S. He has presented to the Ministry of Health a plan to pay the Iraqi Army physician more than their civilian counterparts. That did not go well. He argued that if these men are putting their lives on the line, then the increased cost to provide care would be worth the cost, and I agree with him.

When the Surgeon General heard the presentation of what we are doing now to take care of the detainees, he commented that they are getting better medical care than they can offer to their Army or civilians. We have 13,500 detainees at two locations. Our medical people taking care of the detainees see 3500 appointments a week. They individually dispense the meds for 24,000 doses given a week. The detainees line up and our medical personnel watch that the detainee takes their medicines at each dosing.

Their army is also getting stronger. We heard of how the Mosul group stood up to a large group of insurgents recently, where they had fled before. A similar thing happened in the south where about 600 Iraqi Army fought a group of 6000 anti-Iraqi fighters and the Iraqi Army won the battle, though they took casualties. Thirteen of their men fought in one area until their ammo was spent, and were captured and then assassinated. Instead of dissuading the Army, it inspired them to fight on for their lost friends. They are able to fight now because they are better trained and better equipped, so things are gradually changing.

Our mission is now changing to one of supporting this government and people and not being and doing all for them. They are people of strong character and determination with a long and proud history. The Surgeon General when giving COL Swan, our outgoing commander, a token of appreciation said that he liked history. He taunted a bit by saying that America has only 250 years of history as a country to learn, while they have 7000 years. In that he is correct.

We have helped other countries after we had war with them and they are now world powers, modern and strong, Japan, Korea, and Germany for example. Perhaps some day there will be a different kind of victory here, another "Victory *with* America," and Iraq could join in that group. I hope the future will be promising for these people, for their children. I hope that the children will soon have some good recent history to learn. I am thankful for good people like the Iraqi Surgeon General, who I can now call my friend.

As I sat outside the hotel, looking over the water toward the big palace, for the first time I felt that this is something I would like my wife and children to see. I felt for I wanted to share the moment with them. Yet, I would not want them to be here, not now. I have hope that someday this might be a place where someone would want to come and visit, and could come and feel safe and secure. (Though, by then this five-star hotel might be too costly for me, so I am taking it in now.)

FLARES AND STRYKERS—
PROTECTION

Before we flew I offered a silent prayer that we would make the trip
safely. My guess is that I wasn't the only one with that petition.
A Stryker with a caution sign written in three languages.

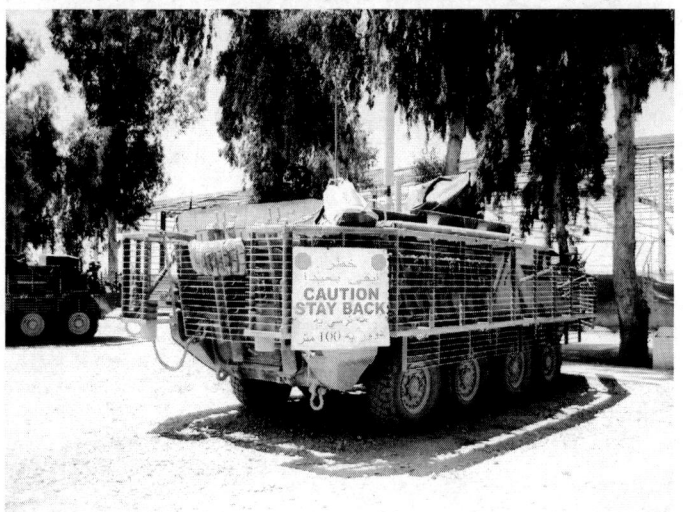

17 Sept. 2006

Dear family and friends,

This week has been a good week for me. I flew back from Baghdad, though that was a small adventure. We loaded onto the C130 aircraft, facing each other in tight quarters. We were packed with heads on the outside and legs facing each other in nearly an overlapping fashion into somewhat of a sardine loading configuration. The plane lifted off and we left Baghdad heading north toward Mosul. After quite some time I heard a funny sound from outside the aircraft, a mechanical sound of moving parts, and wondered what that was. The sound was repeated in a few seconds. The answer came soon. The flares had spontaneously been launched and the crew began taking corrective action. We could not land in a combat zone without flares, so they turned the big bird and headed south to Kuwait.

The one-hour flight had turned into about a three-hour flight. I anticipated a long wait in Kuwait, not knowing even if we would have to spend the night there. Atypical for an Army situation, we were not there very long at all. New flares were loaded, the system checked and we got back in for a ride to Mosul.

The reason the flares fired was not known. There was no attack or threat reported. In our case, it probably was a faulty wire as compared to anything else more exciting, which is fine with me.

I didn't feel bad at all about the delay, didn't even feel irritated, which is against my usual impatient nature. Before we flew I offered a silent prayer that we would make the trip safe. My guess is that I wasn't the only one with that petition. I doubt that we were ever in any danger, but we remained safe. You never know, but perhaps the accidental flare firing was due to a guardian angel triggering the firing devise for something that could have happened, but did not. I trusted in the Lord and we are safe and that is good enough for me.

Back at "home" in Mosul there had been admissions to the hospital from a VBIED meeting a Stryker. A VBIED is a Vehicle Borne IED, a car full of explosives driven by an intended homicidal driver. The Stryker is a kind of army tank on rubber wheels. The Stryker unit from Ft. Lewis is here and three crew members were inside. The explosion was powerful. The sudden powerful impact was followed by heat, flames, shrapnel and body parts flying all over. The Stryker was crushed in and taken out of commission, but inside its crew was intact. There were minor injuries from the jarring and moderate concussions from the blast, but three men walked out alive.

These men were admitted and are doing well. They were discharged back to their work, thankful to be alive and certainly aware that their lives had been spared by the shield of the Stryker vehicle. Had they been in a lesser vehicle, the outcome would have been much different.

The next day the exact story was repeated, another VBIED, another Stryker, another three men were admitted for observation and treatment of minor injuries. Because of the strength of the Stryker, these three men's lives had also been saved. We were told that three Iraqi civilians who were near the explosion and impact were killed, but our men were okay. Our men recognized that they were lucky to be here. The would-be homicidal bombers this time were suicidal bombers and did not take down their intended targets. The Stryker vehicle saves lives. They are a moving fortress against the enemy.

In our lives sometimes we need protection as well. Sometimes there are fiery darts of the adversary who would take us down. Sometime we are bombarded with temptation or evil which could ruin our lives if we were to let it in. Sometimes we are exposed to target rockets which would hit our vulnerable areas if we are not protected. There may be confusion if we do not know the right way. We need flares to drop and divert or confuse the attack away. We need the safety of an enclosed Stryker vehicle against evil. We need a shield to fend off the would-be attack. We need to be inside a protective fortress.

The gospel of Jesus Christ for me is that Stryker vehicle, that fortress which moves with us, which can and will protect us if we rely upon the Lord. I feel to echo the words of the Psalmist. "For the Lord God is a sun and shield..." (KJV: Psalms 84:11).

> "In thee, O Lord, do I put my trust: let me never be put to confusion. Deliver me in thy righteousness, and cause me to escape; incline thine ear unto me and save me. Be thou my strong habitation, whereunto I may continually resort; thou hast given commandment to save me; for thou art my rock and my fortress"
>
> (KJV Psalms 71:1–3).

> "I will love thee, O Lord, my strength. The Lord is my rock, and my fortress, and my deliverer; my God, my strength, in whom I will trust; my buckler, and the horn of my salvation, and my high tower"
>
> (KJV Psalms 18:1–2).

"But thou, O Lord, are a shield for me; my glory, and the lifter up of mine head"

(KJV Psalms 3:3).

I am thankful for a safe ride back to Mosul, for the safe protection of some of the Ft. Lewis soldiers by the Strykers from the explosions of those who would do them harm. I am thankful for the shield and fortress who is my Savior, Jesus Christ, who lifts my head each day. I repeat the words of the Psalms, "I will love thee, O Lord, my strength," my rock, my fortress and my deliverer.

THE ARMY CORPS OF ENGINEERS

In total they have finished 833 schools for the Iraqi children including 300 this year alone. An estimated 325,000 students can now attend school. Things are not where we need to be, but there is increased education, health care, security, transportation, water and sanitation, electricity and oil for the people of Iraq.

Programmed Projects

	Planned	Completed
Schools	846	833
Health Clinics	153	27
Hospitals	32	20
Water	438	264
Border Posts	148	144
Police Stations	346	315
Military Bases	80	57
Electrical	483	185
Village Roads	168	93
Railroad Stations	99	82
Fire Stations	79	75
Oil	58	22
Other	251	177
Total Projects	3181	2294

(IRRF, DFI – 16 June 2006)

*Slide from U.S. Army Corps of Engineers
presentation–June 2006*

24 Sept 2006

Dear family and friends,

Another week has passed and it is another week closer to going home. I am looking forward to that a great deal. My dad would say, "one week more and one week less."

Things are starting to change here. The new FAST team is here and the old one has given them their pagers. There are new doctors who have joined us on rounds. Our replacements (for the 47th CSH) won't be here until early next month, but that is coming soon. The days are getting shorter. No longer can you run early in the morning before work rounds in the hospital because of darkness. The stars are still out. The winter constellations including Orion the Hunter greet me when I wake up and go outside. For many of the Americans here, Orion is greeting them for the second time. They are especially ready to go home soon. The nights are getting cooler and so are the days, but it still gets near 100 degrees by midday. Night gets here more quickly as well, and somehow there seems to be less time during the day, not counting the shorter daylight hours.

Our little church group has gotten smaller as some of the people have redeployed. One of our leaders, Brother John Blandamer, who covers this region—the Arabian Peninsula, has recently gone home. I met him shortly after I got here when he was visiting and then again when he came to see us, the week before he went home. He had been able to meet with most of the servicemen's groups across Iraq and I was curious as to how he was able to travel and do that. He had an administrative job with the Army Corp of Engineers, and traveled the country supervising different projects they have been working on.

The day after he visited our group, I had lunch with him and three other members of his team of the Army Corp of Engineers and learned some really interesting things. They have been very busy in the last few years and especially in the last year. They have traversed the country often, as had John Blandamer, and none of them, nor any of their corps have been injured. They have been blessed to be safe as they have traveled and worked in the communities to make Iraq a better place.

This year they have finished over 800 projects and about twice that many overall. They employ many local workers in the building of these projects and running them after they are completed with over 44,000 Iraqi individuals now employed.

In total they have finished 833 schools for the Iraqi children including 300 this year alone. An estimated 325,000 students can now attend school. The schools are not large and elaborate as you might think of a school in the United States with lunch rooms, gyms, labs, etc. They consist of 12 rooms, one for each grade, and very few other amenities. They have restrooms, but no cafeteria. The teachers have a small lounge. Running water is often only for washing and toilets. Drinking water I assume is bottled, the same as what we drink here.

The schools are most often filled very quickly. The rooms are big enough for 30–35 students per room. Often the local area will donate chairs and possibly tables, with very few desks. The students attend a half of a day and a second group of students comes in the other half. Some of the schools even have three rotations in a day, all taught by the same teachers. Certainly education will be one of the most effective tools this country can use to promote freedom and progress and we are helping make that happen. Boys and girls can now learn to read and write, and learn how to improve their world.

The Army Corps of Engineers have built 27 health clinics and 20 hospitals in the communities. There often are not enough doctors to staff them, but nurses or others with some experience in health care staff them as best as possible. Doctors are currently a rare commodity in the country, but hopefully that will change as the country becomes safer. Some of the clinics have been targeted by bombs as they were being built. They just start over and eventually finish the project and move on. The problem has occurred occasionally with the schools.

They have also worked on digging wells, providing safe drinking water, extending electricity and wiring to places which have not had it before. Over 4 billion dollars have been spent to improve the electricity delivery to the people. 185 electric stations have been built. There is power now available to 1.4 million homes and distributed to 279,000 homes already. This is about 1/3 higher than the pre-war power level. They have build 264 public works and water projects and more and more people have drinkable water. Agricultural projects have benefited from the water distribution as well. The water projects have benefited 1.4 million Iraqi people.

They work on roads and bridges. They have completed 93 roads, 82 railroad stations, 25 fire stations and 144 border posts to help provide security for the country.

There is increased oil production and delivery to the people of Iraq. They have finished 22 oil related projects.

They are helping train police and over 10,000 police cadets have been trained.

They have done all of this at less than one-third of the World Bank estimated cost to make these things happen.

Things admittedly are not perfect in Iraq. In spite of the good things there is much bad here. People and children are not safe. In some places schools have been shut down because families fear for the safety of the lives of their children. People are still being killed and violence is ongoing. But we are headed in a good direction at least in some areas.

Things are not where we need to be, but there is increased education, health care, security, transportation, water and sanitation, electricity and oil for the people of Iraq.

The private sector has benefited from these projects. Many Iraqi people are working and building their dignity and self-esteem. The children are being better educated and the sick are being better taken care of. None of these areas are complete. In fact, in many cases things are just starting, and hopefully things will get better for Iraq, the Middle East, and for our troops and the world.

My thanks this week is to John Blandamer who taught me about the things that have happened and are happening, and to the Army Corps of Engineers, his team, who are making this happen. My thanks go to the Iraqi men and women who teach school, man the clinics and work at the power stations and especially the police stations. Many of the patients in our hospital are or have been Iraqi police. Also my thanks go to the American people who are helping make these changes happen in this part of the world, this part of my world for now, and this part of our world. Perhaps you didn't know you were doing so much good here. Thanks to you.

THE HIGH PRICE WE PAY

We have seen way too many soldiers brought into the hospital.
Yet, have only seen a small percentage of the total killed in Iraq.

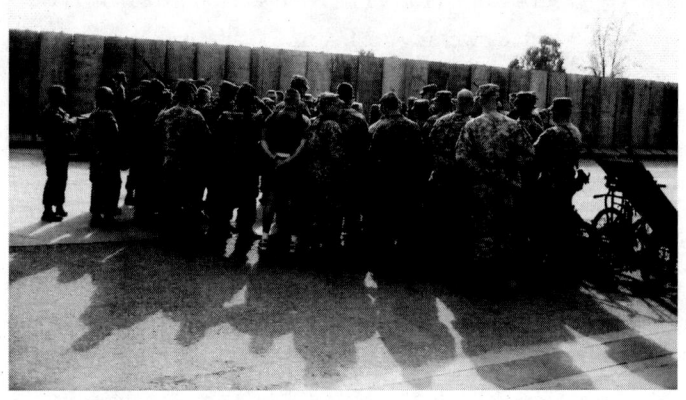

Soldiers gather to pray in tribute to a fallen comrade

25 Sept. 2006

Dear family and friends,

Today I am sick to my stomach as I have been too many times during this short deployment. A young American troop was brought to our Emergency Medical Treatment department after being hit in the side of his head by a sniper. He was breathing on his own when he arrived in his Stryker with a young medic taking care of him. There was a large group who came with him, concerned unit leaders, team members, chaplains, and more became concerned as a very skilled medical team went to work to save his life.

His wounds were bad, but not immediately fatal. The bullet had gone in and out the side of his head. Had the shot been one inch further out he would not have been injured. There was hope that he could be saved. Doctors and nurses and techs surrounded him. IVs were started. Medicines were given to reduce swelling in his brain. He was intubated to protect his airway. He was wrapped to keep him warm, packaged as we say and put on a helicopter, accompanied by a senior anesthesiologist. He was sent to Balad, a forty-minute flight away, where a neurosurgery team was waiting.

He did not make it.

Last week a young female second lieutenant MP was also killed. She was in a HUMVEE and was hit by a homicidal driver of a car bomb. The HUMVEE [High Mobility Multipurpose Wheeled Vehicle] did not protect her like the Stryker's had done for others the week before, saving soldiers. I was upset to my stomach that day. Losing a young man is bad, but somehow losing a young lady seemed worse. Each single loss is the most terrible possible loss to the many people that care and pray for that one soldier; to a parent, a spouse, a sibling or a child.

We have seen way too many soldiers brought in to the hospital. Yet, we have only seen a small percentage of the total killed in Iraq. We have seen victims of IEDs, of car bombs, of homicidal (suicidal) madmen. We have seen children and girls and men who have been killed and injured. We have seen when insurgents give guns to ten- and twelve-year-old boys and tell them to shoot at the Americans and end up injured themselves. We have seen injured Americans, Iraqi and those from other countries who are here. We have seen broken bones, exposed intestines, and pools of blood. We have seen shrapnel wounds and burns covering small areas or most of the body. We have seen ears burnt off and fingers amputated and tendons exposed from the burns. We have fought to save lives and have done so, but not always. We have seen the craft of the sniper. We have seen sniper victim after victim over a period of time. The Iraqi police caught at least one of them for sure a few weeks ago, but there are more out there. We found that out today.

Perhaps it is because I am in the medical profession, perhaps it is because of my religious beliefs, or just my not having someone I consider a personal enemy, but I do not really understand how or why one human being would willfully take the life of another. I do not understand how a sniper can shoot a man in the head as if he were shooting a target. Unfortunately some of them have very good aim.

I most often feel that we are doing much good here in Iraq, not only for the people here, but for the world and the future. I feel that much good is being done by our presence, by our soldiers and by those who support them. I would like to feel that I have done some good in my time here. I have written of some of the good that I have seen. I have seen thankful hearts and received handshakes, hugs and kisses from Iraqi men as is their custom. I have felt a deep love for many of these people.

I also have felt moments of anger and hate and a desire to somehow see the senselessness end. Today, for a time I wondered, as I saw this young soldier being wheeled out to the helicopter knowing that he probably would not make it, if it is really worth it. Is the loss of one of our young men or women worth the price? Freedom is not free. We are free because of the brave. We have heard the slogans, and they are true. Today I was reminded of that. Today I saw a very brave young man who sat in a Stryker, exposed to potential danger because he had courage to try to do the right thing. It was his job and unfortunately he paid with his life.

He was a good young man. I did not know him, but I could tell that those who did knew that. They were concerned for his life. One of them commented that he was a very good man. They loved him as a brother. You could see it in their eyes. They also had in their eyes, I believe, some fear and realization that the next person could be them. Nevertheless, they will go on. Someone else will take his place at the top of the Stryker. Every soldier who goes out on the streets in this war may be facing the last day of his life. I am thankful to him, but mostly I pray that he, whoever he is, will be safe. I do not want to be sick to my stomach again. I do not want a family, a parent, a spouse, a child to get the news that another soldier was killed and this time it is theirs. Today, someone will get that news. May the Lord bless them.

I have to believe that somehow the Lord is over what is happening here. Somehow what we are doing is His will and that it will make a difference to the world, to our children and to the children of Iraq. I really believe that it will. The price is very high, let me assure you. Without that belief, I don't think I could stomach another loss.

WE WIN THE HEART OF A FATHER

He commented to me through an interpreter that his whole feelings and understanding about the Americans and what we were doing changed to the positive.

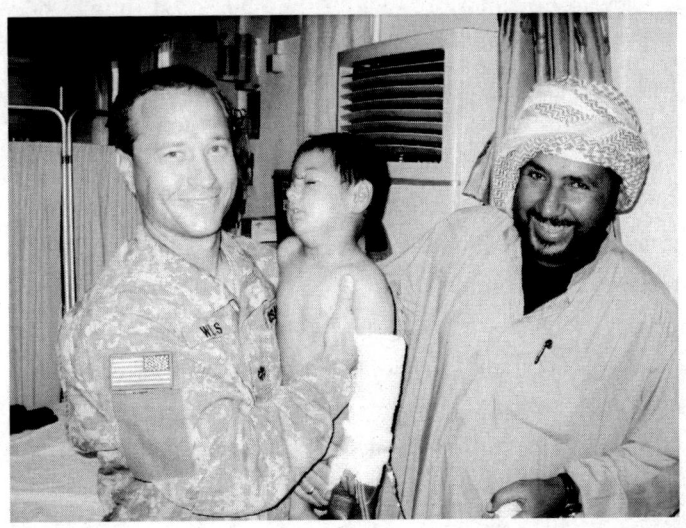

Dr. Wills, our patient and his father

7 Oct. 2006

Dear family and friends,

Another week has passed in Iraq. I have much I would like to write. It has been an "active" week. It is Ramadan for the Muslims here. They fast from morning until evening for a month. That shows significant self-control.

Unfortunately this religious time also seems to bring out some of the radical Muslims as well, and there has been an upsurge of violence, IEDs, car bombs, homicidal (suicidal) bombers, etc. It is a dangerous time in Iraq. We have been busy.

One day we had 9 severe traumas. Five of them came in at once. Some said that there had been small arms fire, but the injuries were shrapnel injuries and so it was obvious that there was an explosion. One of the injured (all Iraqis) said he thought it was a mortar, something shot from far away. Another rumor was that someone had strapped a bomb to his body and set it off in their midst. As we examined the patients some were hurt more than others.

One man lost a foot because it was terribly injured. A tourniquet probably saved his life, and the surgeons finished the job of amputation. Another also had a bad tib-fib fracture or broken lower leg, but his could be repaired. One man did not seem badly injured, but had a curious bone sticking out of his upper thigh. X-ray revealed that his own femur and pelvis were intact. It was a piece of rib, most likely from the one who had set off his explosive vest and so we know how this happened.

A bit later another group of three came in. These were also Iraqis. As I helped get them off of the Ambulance, one was obviously not with us and so one more was added to the casualty list. This time the cause was a Vehicle Borne IED. One said that he could not see out of his left eye, and so we planned on sending him to the ophthalmologist in Balad, but the weather was bad. We have been having bad sand storms recently. By now the surgeons were tired and the ICU was getting full. A CT revealed a foreign body in the orbit of this victim's eye, but his eye globe was intact and by the next day he was doing a bit better. We discussed his care with the ophthalmologist who reviewed the CT electronically and he elected not to do surgery, so we continued to treat his eye as far as infection and his other wounds. He was my patient. Another in the ICU had a similar problem, with jaw fractures as well. He will not see again from his injured eye since his globe was severely damaged.

One of my friends, Dr. Alex Niven, commented to me as I was walking down the hall after the two groups of patients that I didn't have the usual spring in my step. I replied that we had just seen several people injured and one killed and that there was reason to be a bit more somber. He agreed that I was correct.

A few minutes later, we got a call that another patient was on a helicopter from Tal Afar. Another trauma was being brought in and it was a child, a three-year-old. They paged me, but I had not gone far. The story this time was a bit different. The child had wandered out into a field and had been kicked by a donkey in her face. She was bleeding, the eye swollen and the child was unconscious. One pupil was larger than the other and this could indicate a serious brain injury. The family took her to a health clinic and was told that they could do nothing for the child, so she was then taken to the local hospital and again were told that nothing could be done. In desperation the family took the child to the Americans near their town.

The child was examined. The left pupil was markedly dilated. She was poorly responsive. They called in an air evacuation helicopter from Tal Afar. An IV was started and the child was wrapped in a blanket, placed on a stretcher and sent along with her father. When they arrived, the Emergency Department was just being cleaned from the last patients. The child was somewhat responsive, but would not open her eyes. As we opened them we noted that the pupils were markedly different and her left eye seemed very painful. We sedated her, managed her airway and sent her to the CT scanner.

At last we had some good news, her CT scan did not show any fractures and her brain was normal. There was no swelling, no bleeding, no evidence of significant trauma. Clearly the child had a bad concussion, but she should recover. The different size pupils were most likely from the trauma to the eye. We have an optometrist here, so he evaluated the eyes with a slit lamp and found a corneal abrasion, or a scratch on the clear part of the eye. This is generally very painful, but treatable, and so we treated the eye. She did have a large laceration over her left eye and on her nose. I thought of who would be the best to sew this up. MAJ Brandon Wills, a very skilled Emergency Room physician from Madigan and a good friend of mine, took the task and did an exceptional job.

The little three-year-old's name was Sallee and her father was exceedingly pleased with everything that had happened from the helicopter flight down, to the CT scan, the suturing, and also for the good news. He was very impressed and thanked us over and over. He commented to me through an interpreter that his whole feelings and understanding about the Americans and what we were doing changed to the positive. I asked him to share what he had found and experienced with others that perhaps the fighting could stop. He replied, "I wish it would, to God that it would."

I think that it is through actions like this that we can change the hearts and minds of the people over here. The one thing that I regret about my time here is our inability to do more humanitarian work. The command has not allowed this because things are not safe. If we opened the doors to let the Iraqi people come more freely onto the FOB and into the hospital, we would do much good for them and for our country and its image. We would also expose more people and ourselves to the crazies, the fanatics and to possible homicidal bombers and the like. Yet I am thankful that we got to treat this one little girl from the country and change the heart of a young Iraqi father.

CRIBBAGE

This war is like a big game of cribbage in some ways, but the stakes are not bragging rights but life, freedom, hope, and the pursuit of happiness

Dr. Lee sees one of our patients in Iraqi follow-up clinic. This young boy lost his arm in an ambush.

Dear family and friends,

It's Friday and time to play a game of cribbage with my next door neighbor and friend, Dr. Greg Lee. Dr. Lee is perhaps the busiest surgeon here, as he is an orthopedic surgeon and most of our trauma involves the extremities, the legs and arms. He puts the bones back together and is very good at what he does. Recently I helped him reconstruct the end of the humerus, or upper arm. He basically refashioned the bone for the elbow joint from pieces of shattered bone found in the surrounding tissues and from a large piece of bone cut from the patient's hip. It was a very impressive operation.

Greg and I hit it off as friends shortly after we arrived. I enjoy talking to him, running, having a meal together and recently beating him in cribbage. Cribbage is a game which is not played too often any more. My dad loved it. When Dad was older he played with a good friend and neighbor of ours, Troy Bailey, until Troy passed on. They became best of friends and enjoyed beating each other at the game. They would whoop and holler and laugh and complain. One could hear them from the little trailer a block away. Dad and I often played and he beat me all the time, until I learned the game and then we played pretty evenly.

I saw a cribbage board in the hospital and asked Greg if he wanted to learn. He did and we have become competitors, in a friendly way as we play on most days if there is time. Actually we have played enough that he has learned the game and now beats me as often as I beat him. It is a fun thing to do and helps pass the time. We laugh and holler when we win, and complain when the cards are not coming our way. The game has caught on and I have taught others. I have also found others who also love the game and now it is being played often in our area.

Cribbage is a counting game. You look for cards that add to 15. When you play cards that add to 15 you get two points. You count up to 31 on alternate plays and then start over. You peg as you get 15 or 31, or runs or pairs. You take turns getting an extra hand of cards and points called the crib. You take turns cutting a card which is counted with your hand and the crib. If you win by 90 you "skunk" your opponent. That counts as winning two games if you kept account. Greg has skunked me a few times and that especially makes his day. In the end, if you know how to play, it is the cards which really are boss. If you get good cards, you will likely win, and if you do not, you will likely lose. Some games are close and in the end making the right decisions determines the winner, but that is not always the case.

In life we are dealt different cards. Sometimes we get great hands and get on some kind of a run or streak where for some reason it seems almost impossible to lose. All the cards we cut or turn up help us. Things are good and we sometimes feel that we are pretty good players in this thing called life. We win, perhaps we even "skunk" our challenges, whether they be an opponent or a personal goal. We might even get a bit proud in our luck.

But eventually, at least most often, the cards will turn and then we lose. We can't make a hand, can't get a cut, or make the right choice. Every move turns out to be wrong and we get down, feel like a loser, or become depressed. The turns of life might be a deployment where we are away from our families, an illness, an accident or a hundred things. Here people are faced with bombs, burns, shrapnel wounds, loss of their arms or legs or a death of a family member. They are displaced from their homes and worry about their children being safe, their spouses and their own lives. They worry about making a living and feeding their families. They worry about their future and where life will take them and their country. They don't see many good cards turning up for them, and yet they hope and do what they can to get through the hard times.

Life doesn't have to be perfect, but like cribbage or any other card game, the cards most often turn and if you are patient you will win again and laugh and enjoy the game of life. If you continue on doing your best, then there will be success. There will be times when you make a great finish when you thought you were beat. There will be times when you can enjoy family and friends and just the challenges of day to day living.

This war is like a big game of cribbage in some ways, but the stakes are not bragging rights but life, freedom, hope, and the pursuit of happiness. We and the people in Iraq are in a war together, not playing a game, but we hope for a victory. We hope to help them to be able to win the game of life. We hope they will be able to have peace, national and personal security and that we will be able to return to our homes and lives. We hope that they will be able to feed their children, be gainfully employed and build their country. We hope that there will be freedom here, freedom to make choices, to worship as they desire and to let others worship as they feel is right. We are fighting for their children to be educated, to not live in ignorance and fear. We are fighting for them to grow up and someday have their own homes, families, jobs and dreams, and that our own children will be safe to have those things. We are fighting so they can enjoy their own games and can laugh and know what it is to win and to lose because of bad luck and not because of insurgents and terrorists who desire to take away these freedoms.

I am thankful for good friends like Greg Lee, for cribbage games and for the enjoyment that comes from a good game. I am thankful for my father and mother, who taught me how to play games including the game of life. They taught me to want to win and to accept and learn and grow from the losses. And that is worth two points.

GOD'S WILL

This had happened and it must have been God's will. God is in charge and it was God's will. It was his son's time. It was okay.

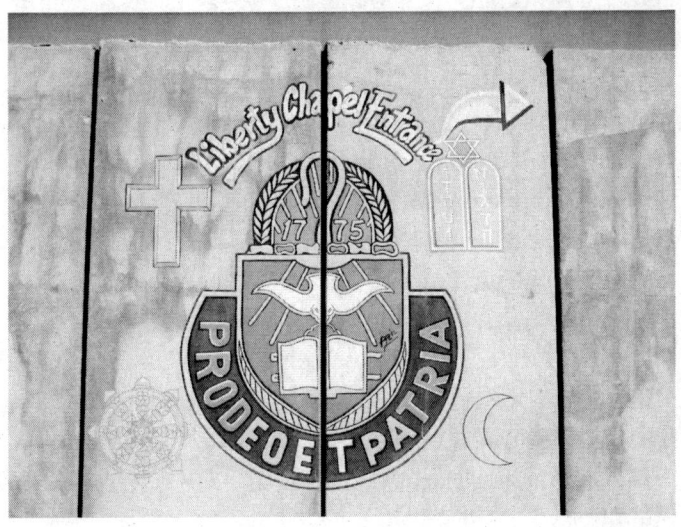

Painted T-walls outside the chapel in Mosul

8 Oct. 2006

Dear family and friends,

Yesterday was another long day. By the end of the day we had sent four people to the morgue. This included an Iraqi woman of about 40 who was killed by an IED early in the morning, a seven-year-old who was killed by a car bomb, a 14-year-old who was shot in the head and an American soldier who was killed in the early evening. The American had been killed as his Stryker ran over an IED and was sent tumbling. He was tossed within the Stryker, hitting his neck and head. He died immediately.

When the 14-year-old arrived, his head was bandaged and he was working hard to breath. He was not responsive to any stimulation. He was bleeding badly. There was a puddle sign below his head on the floor. His heart was strong. He was taken to the CT scanner where the degree of trauma was fully assessed. He would not survive the injury. No surgery could repair the damage. From the CT scanner he was taken to a room where a kind nurse stayed at his side, gently talking to him and touching his young face. I do not believe that he was aware of this, but her compassion for him and life was clearly evident. The chaplain came by and offered a prayer which was in accordance to the Muslim faith. The nurse stayed with him, cleaned him up, until his breathing weakened and his heart stopped. I was there as well, and my mind was racing, my feelings churning. The seven-year-old boy's body also lay covered, across the room on a gurney.

I could not believe that a 14-year-old would be shot in the head. I thought first of the enemy sniper and wondered what had happened. I began to ask about. There were various stories of what had happened, but none first hand, and none seemed reliable. The thing that became clear was that we, the Americans, had shot the young man. Some thought that he was driving a car toward the Strykers and did not respond to warning shots. Such a person would be assumed to be driving a VBIED (car bomb) with a plan to destroy the Stryker. He seemed too young to be driving. Nothing made sense.

After a time we had word that his relatives were at the gate and were being escorted in. We didn't know exactly who was coming, but there were two of them, perhaps his parents. Being a pediatrician and senior physician I was asked to talk to them through an interpreter. We arranged a room for our conversation. It was the same room where he had passed away. As we brought chairs into this room I noticed drops of blood on the floor. This would not be good, so I wiped them up, cleaning up a bit of the evidence of what had happened. What would I say? What could I say?

Soon they arrived. They were introduced as an uncle and his father. The father was a bit older than I had suspected and was dressed in a brown long Iraqi garment, a Throbe, which they wear. Sasha, one of our interpreters, joined COL Jose Stout, the DCCS (Deputy Commander of Clinical Services) of the hospital, the chaplain and me in the room. Introductions were made. As we had them sit down and started to talk, they waved their hands and indicated that they only wanted to know that the teenager was alive and that they wanted everything done for him.

I let them know about the wounds he had incurred and that his brain had been terribly injured. I then let them know that he had in fact died. There was pain easily visible in their faces and in their posture to the news, but no anger seemed to be expressed. They said that the shot had been an accident and it was obvious that they were indeed in pain for the loss. It almost seemed to me that death had become an expected part of their culture. We expressed our sorrows and told them that a full investigation would take place. I asked the boy's name and said that he looked like a healthy good kid. They said it was Hali and that he was a good kid. It was his second day to be able to take care of the sheep by himself, and that apparently was where he was going, on foot.

They wanted to see the body and later to recover the body. They did not know what they were going to do. The father was Shiite and had been displaced from his own home with his family. He had lived near the Syrian border and with the change in power had lost his home to the Kurds and came to live with his brother in Mosul.

The uncle decided to leave, to go and tell the family. The father would stay to take care of things and recover the body. He would need to talk to Civil Affairs. They were called and we began to wait for them. Gradually, the others who were there left and soon it was just the father and I sitting there. We moved to the front lobby where the Civil Affairs officers would come and began waiting. We waited for some time. I wanted to talk, to ask questions, to share my feelings again. But we sat there quietly. People came through the door and greeted me, soldiers and former patients. Saturday afternoon Iraqi clinic and former Iraqi patients come back for follow-up. Several came through and we exchanged greetings, some handshakes, some hugs. A young boy who had suffered a spinal cord injury came through. He was doing much better, now able to walk without assistance. These Iraqis had survived their injuries. I thought of this man's young son, now gone.

The wait turned out to be very long, much over an hour. I apologized in gestures to this father. He wanted to go for a walk and we did. He wanted to go out and smoke a cigarette and so he did, crouched and sitting on the ground in the shade of a barrier. It was a hot day out there and he was fasting for Ramadan. He wouldn't take anything to drink.

Eventually several people arrived, to include the Stryker unit who had fired the shots. The commander, an experienced captain, began to talk to the father, expressing his sorrow. He told the interpreter that it had been one of his men who had been responsible for the shooting. There was pain in his eyes and face. Before the interpreter could get out even a few words, the Muslim father stopped her and replied that he held no one responsible. This had happened and it must have been God's will, *"En sha la."* God is in charge and it was God's will, *"En sha la."* It was his son's time. It was okay. I was taken back. The captain was taken back. The others there heard what was said.

We again said that we were extremely sorry for the loss and understood that the boy could not be replaced. The father was given a sum of money to help take care of things, for the funeral and arrangements. It was made exceedingly clear to him that the money was not to replace the son, but to help out.

I asked the captain how his soldier who had fired the shot was doing and what had happened. He told me that the soldier was there, standing, watching, listening to what had been said. He was a new squad leader. He was a 1st Lieutenant and he looked like he was just a kid himself. He looked sick. You could see that he felt terrible inside.

He told me that a car had been coming up on the Stryker. Alarms were sounded. On the back of the Strykers is a big sign that says "Stay Back" in three languages. Warning shots were fired into the ground in front of the car. The car did stop and turned around. No one in the car was hurt. To their horror they then saw that a young boy had been hit. They turned around to pick him up and get help. The young soldier had not seen the boy when he fired. The youth had been hit by a random bullet, a ricochet from the ground. It was no one's fault, and certainly had not been intentional. I understood that this was an accident rather than a mistake and suddenly I felt much better. It had been witnessed by the Iraqi people and thus I understood that the father apparently already knew the rest of the story.

I think the father's response had to be somewhat comforting to this young soldier. The father did not know that the responsible shooter was standing across from him, did not know that the rifle that could have fired the shot was being held just a few feet from him. He did not care.

I thought of the Iraqi's response, that this had been God's will. *En sha la* they say. "It is up to God," or "God willing." This is common in the Muslim belief as well as the Christian's. Was this death, this accident, really God's will? I wonder about the second child, the 7-year-old whose father and he had been killed by the VBIED and whose uncle would come later in the day to see the body. They were innocently driving by in the father's taxi when a sudden explosion took their lives. Was this God's will? I thought of many of my patients who have died of their cancers as children. Was this and is this God's will? How could this Muslim be so accepting of this as God's will? How could he have enough faith to accept everything that happens around him as "God's will"? Where was my faith and trust in God as sovereign? Does everyone have "a time"? Was it this boy's time yesterday? What this stray bullet meant to be?

As physicians, can't we change what would happen to injured and sick people? The cure rate for childhood cancers is going up and up. More children who would have died of their disease are now living. Are we making the changes, or is God making the changes? Is God allowing us to move forward for a reason? Certainly I believe that God provides the cure. Two patients with exactly the apparent same disease will respond differently. One will live, and one will die. It is not in my power to save one over the other. I provide the same treatment. Is this God's will?

When a child get cancer, the family will often ask, "Why? Why did this happen?" When a child's cancer comes back, they ask the same question. What is God's will"? These are questions I can not answer. I do not know the answer. I do not believe that God wills a child to get cancer, but I do not know. His ways are higher than our ways. His thoughts are higher than our thoughts. He knows the end from the beginning, for He is all knowing, all powerful, sovereign, over and above all things.

I do believe that God is fully aware of the things that happen, of children who get cancer, and that he allows us to be subject to mortality. I believe that He will be there to support and strengthen those who turn to Him in these times. I believe that He will make our experiences, tribulations, trials, and our losses build us and be for our own good if we will trust in Him, have faith perhaps more in "God's will."

I do believe that we have free will. God's foreknowledge does not change our ability to learn, nor our being subject to accidents, to stray bullets and to the random events that lead to cancer. I believe that we have some power over our own destiny, but truthfully we do not know if today will be "our time," if it is "God's will."

I don't know God's will in all things. I don't even know his will in many things, certainly in events that happen in our lives. I do not believe that everything that happens is God's will. I do not believe that people who put on a vest of explosives and walk into a public place and blow up everyone around them as well as themselves is God's will. I do not believe that someone who sets an IED and detonates it at the right moment to kill an innocent lady such as the one who had died yesterday is God's will. Most often many are killed. I do not believe that setting a truck on its side so the police can come and investigate it and then when they do detonating it at the same time a father and his seven-year-old son are driving by is really God's will. The people who do this are not on God's errand, even if they believe they are.

The idea of "God's will" can be carried too far. Someone decides that it may be God's will for them to die as a martyr. They strap explosives to their body and go into a public square and try to detonate them. They think, "If it goes off then it must be God's will, but if it doesn't, then it must not." Such might be the thinking of those who detonate bombs and kill themselves or others.

I do believe though that if we are on God's errand the

things that happen to us are more likely to be God's will. I believe that he is aware of our circumstances, of even the hairs of our head that fall to the ground, of our challenges, our illnesses, and of our faltering and that He will intervene as we are obedient. Sometimes he blesses us, and sometimes he chastises us for our own good.

I admit that I do know God's will in many things. He wants me to have faith in His son, Jesus Christ, to accept Him and always remember Him. I know that he wants me to obey his commandments. He wants me to be kind and forgive others. He wants me to be clean of mind and heart. He wants me to pray to him, to study his word, the scriptures. He wants me to keep His Sabbath day holy. He wants me to give to those who have less than I do, to serve Him through serving others. He wants me to recognize his hand in my life, to recognize His greatness and goodness in the world around me and especially in my life. He wants me to be honest, to be where I should be when I should be there. He wants me to love Him and to love those around me.

I also know that he wants me to not cheat, to not bear false witness, to not steal, to not hate, and to not kill. He wants me to not commit adultery nor do anything like unto it. He wants me to not lust and to not view pornography. He wants me to not commit any sin, though he knows that I will still often fail in my thoughts and actions.

Thus He wants me to repent and to do better. He wants me to keep trying and when I do, he blesses me to change, to improve, to be a bit stronger and better. It is through his love, his grace, and his blessings that I am able to do any of the things that he wants me to do. I do know God's will in many things. I do know his will in who he wants me to be. Perhaps I need to have more faith in God's will in the events around me.

I believe that God's hand is somehow over the things that are happening in the world. I believe that He is in charge and that ultimately His will will be done on earth as it is in heaven. I believe that His kingdom will come. If God is over all things, then he is over what is happening in Iraq and will turn this into what he wants it to be. It may take time, a few or many years. Walls have fallen, iron curtains have been removed, and who can doubt God's will in those things. Why can we not see God's will here in Iraq?

Christ prayed in that great atoning prayer in the Garden that not his human will but that God's will would be done. When we pray, we should do the same, not to give God instructions, but that we might live and do according to God's will. We should pray for things that we believe to be God's will. We can pray for safety and blessings, for God will give good gifts to those who ask. It is his will to bless us. We can pray that nations will be changed, that hearts will change. We can pray for others, for health, for miracles, but we too must remember, not our will "but thine be done."

Remember the country song that some of God's greatest gifts are unanswered prayers, or what we see as unanswered. In those cases, perhaps we were praying for our own will and not for God's will.

I am thankful for God's will for me, though I must trust and have faith in what happens today and what will happen tomorrow. I am thankful for this Iraqi parent who showed that he has great trust in God's will. *En sha la.*

MY TOUR COMES TO AN END

From what I observed, it is my opinion that the patients could not have received better care at any trauma center in the world.

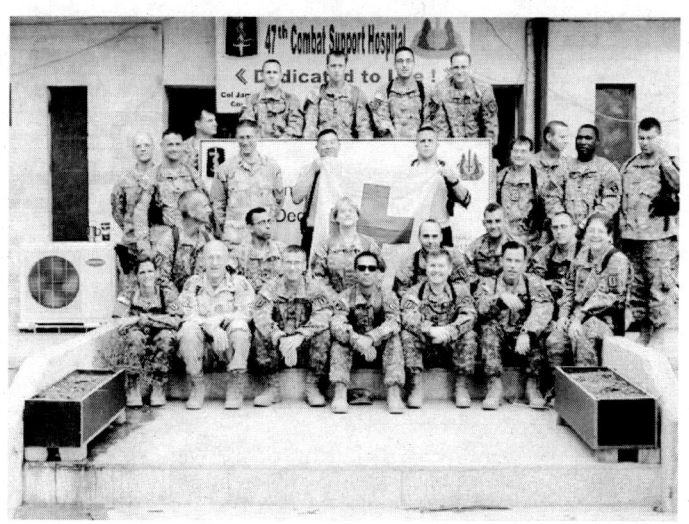

The group of physicians from the 47ᵗʰ CSH–Sept. 2006

18 Oct. 2006

Dear family and friends,

What can I say at the end of it all, at least at the end of my deployment adventure? I am sure my experience in Iraq is unique, as is every soldier's who serves there. On the other hand, we have many shared experiences. One thing that I came away with, which is common to most all soldiers, is a common bond with my co-workers. I have made friends that I hope will last for years. Others experiencing the same thing as you quickly become your brother and sister.

Working in the hospital, I was able to see the worst of what had happened, though after the fact. I also was able to see perhaps some of the best that happened. I was able to witness firsthand, heroes, compassion and the struggle for life. Hearts were softened, minds changed and doors opened. This would not have happened had we not been there.

There were so many experiences that I thought I should write down, and many of those have slipped from my immediate memory. There are things that I was able to write to you and in my journal. I hope that the things that I have written have been in someway helpful to the reader.

As five of the 250 of us who flew from Kuwait to El Paso were flying from El Paso to San Diego in our uniforms the stewardess announced that on board were soldiers who had served in Iraq. The plane broke out into a spontaneous applause. My eyes filled with small tears from that applause and support. Applause again happened as we touched down at SeaTac Airport when a similar announcement was made. Many en route home said to us, "Thanks for serving." Many offered their hands and shook ours.

I know that there are many people in this country who do not support the war, do not support the fighting, and do not support the loss of Americans in Iraq. Yet almost everyone supports those American soldiers who put their lives on the line to do their duty and to serve so selflessly.

I was lucky to have served only 6 months there, while most are away from family and friends for a year and even longer. Many had their time serving there extended. Being away for that time was not easy, but for me it ended as an enlightening experience and a positive chapter in my life.

For the last 6 months I was able to be a part of history. The survival rate for injuries in this war, for the 30th medical brigade, our command, is documented as the best of any war in history. If someone was injured, their chance of surviving was better than any other time in the past. The medical care which was provided to our soldiers and to the men of the Iraqi army and police and the civilians we took care of was world class. From what I observed, it is my opinion that the patients could not have received better care at any trauma center in the world. Their chance of survival could not have been better any other place than that which was provided at the 47th CSH in Mosul, Iraq. It will be very difficult for the next CSH, the 399th Reserves from Massachusetts, to match that level of care.

The medical care started on the battlefield. The injured were found bleeding and burnt. The bleeding was stopped or slowed with special clotting bandages and with tourniquets applied in a skillful manner by young medics and soldiers who were trained in these life-saving techniques. Patients were put into ambulances, into Strykers, into whatever modified vehicles could be put together to get them to the hospital. Helicopters were called in and rapidly flown to the Combat Support Hospital and from there to another facility where they could be given additional neurosurgery or other care. Jet planes took our soldiers, once stable, to Germany and then back to military hospitals in the United States.

In the hospital a patient arrived and was quickly surrounded and evaluated. Intravenous lines were started and precious fluids including blood were given. The airway was secured by intubation if needed. Often after the patient left to the operating room or intensive care unit, a pool of blood was left on the floor. The operating room floor was also often covered with that precious fluid, but the bleeding was stopped.

I saw lives saved by the hands of skilled surgeons, emergency room personnel, and by skilled clinicians. Wounds were bound up, cleaned up and sewn up. I saw skilled nurses, therapists and technicians contribute to the healing. Bandages were changed, medicines given and smiles exchanged. Patients were washed, fed, helped to walk, given hope and allowed to heal.

The statistics speak for themselves. But I also believe that part of the reason the injured did better is that the soldier in battle had been trained to offer appropriate first aid and had the equipment to do so. Importantly, they also were better protected. The body armor and Kevlar helmets saved lives. The armor on the vehicles and the technology used in this war saves lives. The medical care is good, but the protection our soldiers have is also good.

Nevertheless, we continue to see numbers of American Heroes killed in action and by accidents as they serve. The loss of life is not unique to our soldiers, but others who are there from other countries and as civilians have given their lives. Most of all, the Iraqi people are losing fathers, children, mothers and friends at an alarming rate. Many of those killed are on the side of freedom and liberty. Others are insurgents, people who would kill and do kill, sometimes themselves in order to take others' lives. Many kill and are killed because of differences in tribal ancestry, customs, religion and ideology.

We officers had the chance to stand guard for a day in the last week we were there at the hospital, MWR and gym and I took my turn, giving a small token of thanks to the enlisted who do this for hours each week. An Iraqi interpreter came to the gym, where I was working, and we talked of the war for nearly an hour. He commented that the Iraqi were brothers fighting each other as brothers sometimes do. He said that the Americans were there trying to stop the fight, trying to put out the fire which has been lighted in their hearts. He also said that those from Iran, from Syria and other places were there pouring gasoline on that fire. That is a big part of the war. He worries that he will not have a life to go back to because he has sided with the Americans and stepped up and worked to make his country better. You could tell that that decision had been a hard one for him. Also you know that we still have enemies in Iraq.

He understands the need for freedom, freedom to choose, to work and to believe to a certain extent. He is a Muslim and the depths of his belief were evident as he commented that too many young people leave Iraq for that freedom and then leave the Muslim beliefs. You could hear the hurt in his voice as we talked. I feel that myself when I meet someone who has left the faith that I hold so dearly in my heart, so I understand his devotion and pain.

My sendoff from Iraq was not good. The night before we left, we were mortared, with several mortars landing on the base near a new temporary dining facility and hospital. When they started, I was in the MWR getting ready to call family for the last time from Iraq. The calling ended. The blasts kept coming and we were told that we could go to the basement in that building. After just a few minutes of silence, several of us decided to run to the nearby hospital where we worked, in case someone had been injured. As we ran, you could hear small arms fire *rat-a-tat-tat, rat-a-tat-tat* nearby.

There were not yet reports of injuries, but we began to prepare the ward in case some came. The news soon came that there had been injuries and I went back to the emergency department where a patient soon arrived. At first I thought it was a pediatric patient which surprised me, but then realized it was one of the techs that worked in the hospital clinic, who I knew well, Tara Edminson. She is one of smallest soldiers that I know, but is a great young lady with a big heart who had done a great job in the hospital. She was planning on going home in another week. SPC Edminson had to go to the operating room, this time as a patient, but is okay and will recover fully. This is the first injured patient that I knew personally and I hurt for her.

Before the night was over, 11 patients had been brought in, including the young man who had also been close to the blast that hit Tara and who had picked her up and ran with her to get help. He developed some chest pain and had a mild concussion himself. He is a hero for his actions. None were very seriously injured. The last to come in was the only Iraqi patient of the group.

The insurgents who launched the rockets were quickly found in the act and thus the launching stopped. The remaining 2/3 of their mortars were confiscated before they could be launched. The small arms fire resulted in two of the insurgents being killed. Another of them was injured and brought to the hospital for medical care. Many others were captured by the Mosul police, showing the progress they are making. More injuries could have happened and possibly lives been lost, had we not been able to localize the firing location and get there very quickly.

As I am home from Iraq I think of the young soldiers who are there fighting and doing their duty. They are fine young men and young women for the most part. There are those who have made wrong choices as soldiers, but they are the rare exception. I think of them as they give out crayons and soccer balls to the children of Iraq and how they love to see the children, and I am proud. I think of the tenderness given to the children in the hospital by these young soldiers and I am proud. I think of the same care and compassion given to the injured American, to the burnt Iraqi soldier in the hospital, and yes to the injured insurgent, and I am proud.

When I arrived at the SeaTac airport I was greeted by my good wife and daughter, my son-in-law and my granddaughter. It was fantastic to see them again. I watched as Dr. Brandon Wills and Dr. Alex Niven hugged their wives and I was touched. As I turned into our neighborhood the street was lined with 85 full size flags, placed for me by the scouts of my church at the request of my wife. My heart filled to overflowing with love for

America, for my good family, and to be home. I also was thankful for the experiences that I had in Iraq.

For this last time I thank the American people for their support of the American soldier. I thank you, my friends and especially my family for your support while I was gone, for your prayers and thoughts. I thank those of you who sent 110 boxes of items to me to give to the injured soldiers, Iraqi and to the children.

I join with the American people and thank the brave young men and women who are there in harm's way. I thank those who replaced us, those who are there for the second and third time and those going for the first time. I thank those who will yet go, who will leave their families and risk their own lives to help make the world a better place. Some who serve are not so young; some are even older than I am. I thank them all for their heroism, for their honor and valor in virtually all situations.

I thank those of the 47th CSH who so skillfully saved lives. From what I saw there, the American soldier serves with dignity, honor, and yes, even love. We as Americans should be proud of them. In a few months I will likely retire after 28 years of wearing an American uniform. I am honored to be one of them. I am glad to be home.

P.S.—Though I hope to continue to write, this will be the last letter I will send out to this group. If you would like to continue to hear from me, please let me know.

ISLAM

Muhammad initially taught that the Jew and Christian believed in the same God, were all people 'of the book' and that the sword should only be used if they attacked the Muslim.

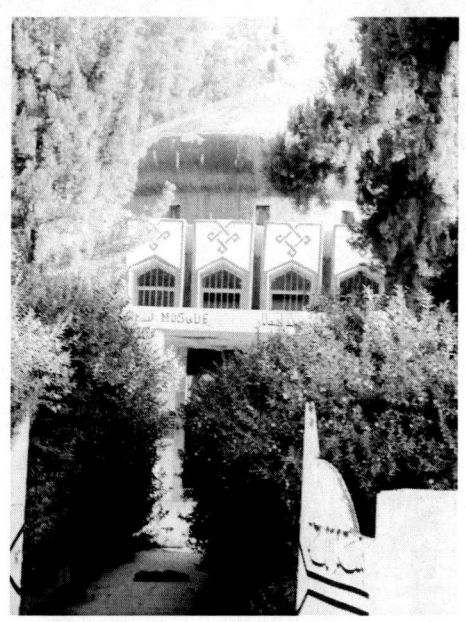

The gate and Mosque on FOB Diamondback

While in Iraq and since coming home I have become interested in learning what the Muslims believe and more about Islam. I wanted to know its beginnings, beliefs and how they relate to other beliefs. Below is a general summary of some of the things I found out. This information is widely available and I believe is accurate.

In the year 570 Mohammad (Muhammad) was born. He became a herder of sheep. The people where he lived had their religion and though Christianity was relatively new it was not established there, or perhaps had become apostate. There were idols and the worship of a plurality of gods.

When Muhammad was 40, he often went to a cave to fast and meditate and there he said that the angel Gabriel visited him and taught him. Gabriel taught him that there was only one God and the name given was Allah. He learned that this was the God of Adam and of Abraham. It was the God of Moses and he also believed that it was the God of Jesus the Jewish prophet. Muhammad had descended from Abraham through Ishmael. He believed that Islam is the oldest of the monotheistic religions, the religion of Adam and Abraham. Interestingly Allah is the name that Arabic Christians use for God, I am told. Muhammad believed that the Christian and the Jew also believed in the same God he believed in.

He began to spread his teachings and formed Islam, which interpreted is "submission to and acceptance of God." A Muslim (also spelled Moslem) is "One who submits to God." He began to lead a small militia of men who fought to overthrow the false teachers of many gods. He did not write down his teachings for he did not know how to write, but they were memorized and passed on to his followers, who memorized them and after some time were written down as the Koran (Quran). The Koran is therefore not so much a book as it is the teachings of Mohammed—of course as remembered and finally recorded by his followers.

These teachings were taken as the "final word" from God and thus the basis for Islam. Mohammed was seen as the final prophet. Subsequent leaders of the group were not equal, but were the keepers of the words of the Koran, the teachings of Mohammed. The religion spread quickly and later was sometimes spread by the sword. There was debate of who should be the leader of this group and over time there were assassinations. After just three successors to Mohammed there was division in the believers.

One group felt that Allah blessed the true believer and as such prosperity, wealth and power were the blessings given the true believers. This is supported by the Sunni belief. The other group believed that the true believers should be humble, give up everything for the cause, be abased or near destitute as the true form of worship. They became the Shiite. Many of the Shiite early leaders were martyred and thus the idea of being a martyr is held as a very high thing. The Sunni have looked down on the Shiite for the subsequent centuries while the Shiite have despised the ideology of the Sunni as proud and vain and thus not correct. Thus Muslims have their "Catholics and Protestant" differences.

Saddam Hussein with his power was a Sunni as might be expected. He looked down upon the Shiite, but in Iraq the majority of the population (65%) were Shiite. In a way it is not surprising that the Baath party of Sunni would rise to power because of their ideology. The Sunni make up 90%

of all Moslems in the world. The Shiite are the majority in Iraq, in Iran, in Lebanon and in the smaller numbers in Azerbaijan and Oman. The rest of world is mostly Sunni. Arab Moslems make up about 18% of all Muslims. There are huge populations of Moslems in Indonesia, and in all of Northern Africa; Morocco, Algeria, Libya and Egypt as well as Turkey and Saudi Arabia of the Middle East. Up to 97% or more of most of these peoples are Islam, and near 100% of them are Sunni. There are 1.4- 1.5 billion Muslims in the world with 1.1 million living in the US.[1]

Muslims believe in life after death and in the resurrection. They do not believe in the Atonement of Jesus Christ, but feel that Allah has power in and of himself to forgive sins. They believe in obedience and that sins such as ignoring God or God's revelations, lying, corruption, denying the resurrection, refusing to feed the poor and indulgence in opulence and exploiting others can consign someone to hell. On the other hand Muhammad taught that if a man had any faith at all, he would be saved, but faith requires faithfulness and the adherence of the heart and performance, particularly the performance of "prescribed duties." They believe in only One God and the first step of belief is a confession that "I testify that there is none worthy of worship except God and I testify that Muhammad is the Messenger of God." They reject the Christian doctrine of the trinity, seeing it as akin to polytheism. God is One and the Only, Eternal, Absolute; He begetteth not, nor is He begotten; and there is none like unto Him. They believe that God is incorporeal, and reject idolatry or visual images or depictions of God. He is Beneficent and Merciful.

There are five pillars or core aspects of Islam. The first,

called Shahadah, is the oral confession mentioned above that there is but one God and Muhammad is his prophet. The second is Salat, or the requirement to pray five times a day at fixed times. These prayers express gratitude and worship God and help restrain one from shameful and evil deeds. The third pillar, called Zakat, is alms-giving or giving charity of at least a fixed portion on one's wealth to the poor and the needy. The fourth is Sawm or fasting, and is done principally during the month of Ramadan. This helps one refrain from violence, anger, envy, greed, lust, harsh language and gossip and to get along better with others. The fifth pillar is Hajj, with is a pilgrimage in the city of Mecca, to be made at least once in the Muslim's lifetime if circumstances allow. Associated with this pilgrimage is a group of rituals and they are done as an expression of devotion to God. They do not eat pork, blood nor ingest alcohol.[2]

The three most holy sites for the Muslim are where Muhammad built Mosques or had significant spiritual experiences. He was a warrior leader and conquered Medda in 630, converting Kabba, believed to have been built by Abraham, into the first Mosque, or place of Islamic worship. He later built a Mosque in Medina and it is said that he talked with God in Jerusalem and ascended into heaven. These most sacred locations therefore include Mecca, Medina and Jerusalem.

Jihad is struggle in the way of God. It is sometimes referred to as the sixth pillar. It has both violent and non-violent meanings, and to some has come to mean "holy war." It may be seen as an armed struggle against persecution and oppression. To some it is also seen as an inner struggle for faith. It is not meant to convert non-Muslims to Islam and Muhammad initially taught that the Jew and Christian believed in the same God, were all people "of the book" and that the sword should only be used if they attacked the Muslim. This happened in the Crusades. Since then, the meaning of the word and fight has taken on a more militant meaning to some, even to the point of the suicidal bomber, willing to kill themselves if they feel that in so doing that Islam will be protected and strengthened.

Muhammad died in 632 at age 62. There was debate about who should be the successor or Caliph. Some tribes felt that their leaders claimed to be prophets and a companion of Muhammad, Abu Bakr, took charge and subdued them in the "Wars of Apostasy." The leader was not seen as a prophet, but as one to carry on Muhammad's message. Subsequent fighting, civil wars and disputations led to the two main sects of the current day Shiites and Sunni as noted above. Tribal disputations have long been a part of the Arab culture. The leadership began to be passed on in families, especially in the Shia denomination, and Islam spread through the Middle East, into Africa, Spain and even China. Persia became Iran. Baghdad became the center of the Shiite empire. The Ottoman Empire eventually was broken up after the First World War and Iraq was formed. As the British Empire formed new countries in the Middle East, they did not always fully consider history, cultural differences and such natural borders.

The Muslim empire believed in education, art and architecture, philosophy and literature and science and technology and led the world for some time. Muslims, like Christians, believe in proselytism and have made converts of many nations and peoples, and have sometimes done so by the sword. If you are not a believer you are seen as an Infidel. The former respect for Jews and Christians as fellow mono-theists following Abrahamic religions has become lost by a large number of Muslims.

In contemporary Islam there are different groups from fundamentalist Islamism to liberal movements and reform-ists. Of the fundamental, groups like the Shiite-led Hezbollah in Lebanon have promoted violence to the point of honoring martyrs who commit suicide. Thiers is a desire to dominate the Middle East with one government, where religion and politics are the same, and to spread throughout the region and world. One of their goals is to destroy Israel and take over their lands which Muslims feel belong to them.

Mohammad and the early Muslim members were descendants of Abraham through his son Ishmael. Ishmael was the first son of Abraham through Sarai's maidservant Hagar. The second son was Isaac. The fighting started even as brothers and as who would have the birthright. God said to Hagar through an angel of the Lord that "I will multi-ply your descendents exceedingly, so that they shall not be counted for multitude. Behold you are with child, and shall bear a son. You shall call his name Ishmael. He shall be a wild man; his hand shall be against every man, and every man's hand against him. And he shall dwell in the presence of all of his brothern" (Genesis 16: 10–12). "God gave them land which would be an everlasting possession" (Gen. 17:8). As for Ishmael again God said, And as for Ishmael, I have heard you. Behold I have blessed him, and will make him fruitful, and will multiply him exceedingly. She shall begat twelve princes, and I will make him a great nation" (Gen 17:20). Yet God's covenant was established with Isaac (vs. 21).

It might be interpreted that Ishmael would be a great nation, but that not only he, but also his descendents would continue to be against every man (every nation) and them against him. Thus the fighting may be a perpetual problem.

The militant Muslim believes that once a land was possessed by the Muslim people, God gave it to them as an everlasting possession. The Jewish people are also descendants from Abraham through Isaac and have the same rights of their lands given to them by God as an everlasting possession. The land of modern day Israel has been possessed by both groups, and thus the fighting goes on.

THE WAR HITS HOME

His memory will never die and the strength of his last battle will build and support his family in their own trials of life.

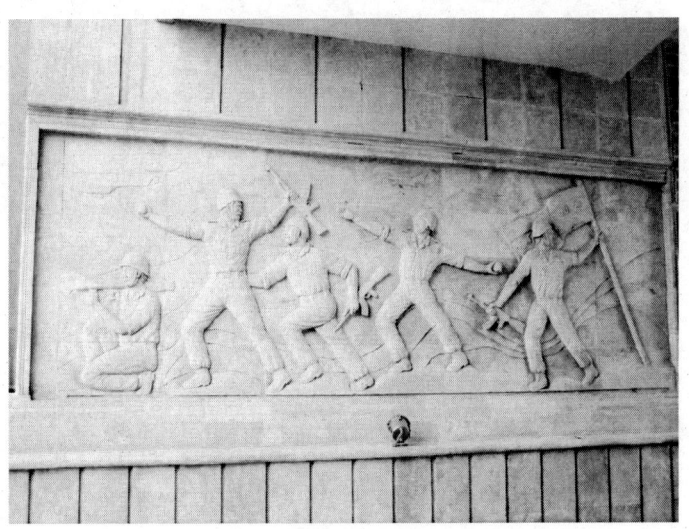

A mural of war fighters on a building at Camp Liberty in Baghdad

21 Dec. 2006

The losses and deaths of the Iraq war hit home in a closer and different way this week. In our pediatric clinic, one of our best nurses, Debbie "K.," who works in the well baby section, lost her husband, Staff Sgt. Henry K. Kahalewai, Jr.; on Dec. 15th. We heard the news during our Christmas party, which we hold in the clinic each year just before the holiday schedule begins. I had to announce it and it really let the air out of our celebration.

On Thursday 21 December a memorial service was held on Ft. Lewis, in the main post chapel. It was well attended by friends, soldiers and by our clinic staff. It was a sobering experience with the same things that have been done for too many soldiers over the last few years.

My wife attended the services of a soldier who I helped with in Iraq who did not make it back to the states, and it was a hard and touching thing for her. She described that service to me, and now I saw those things, symbolically portrayed to honor this great hero who has given his life that the world might be a safer place.

Sgt. Henry Kahalewai is from Hilo, Hawaii, where he was born and where he graduated from high school. He was 43 and was about to retire from the service after 19 years in the military. He had served four tours in Iraq, which is as many as any person that I am aware of. He left his wonderful wife, Debbie, a son and two daughters and a beautiful grandson. He left a father whose name he honored and many friends and comrades who respected and followed him. He joined the military to honor those from Hawaii who had served so valiantly in previous wars. He left Hilo when he was about 25.

He was seriously wounded when a roadside bomb detonated near his Stryker Vehicle Nov. 21, 2006, in Baghdad. He was moved from Baghdad to Balad and then to LRMC in Germany. I recall the day we heard of his injuries. We heard that he had lost his legs, but this was not true. His legs were very injured, broken and torn apart and eventually he had to have one of them removed. We were sick for him and for Debbie. She is one of the hardest workers we have in the clinic and she quietly goes about doing her job with compassion and excellence. He was moved to the states and to Brooke AMC in San Antonio where he fought for his life for two weeks. He developed kidney problems and the ARDS, Adult Respiratory Distress Syndrome, which eventually took his life.

During this time he had his family at his side and he was positive, planning on what he would do when he went home, how life would be and the future he and his family would have. He offered to them wisdom, strength, hope and especially love. The last battle unfortunately was one which he could not win. It was shocking and horrible news that he had finally died from his injuries and the consequences of that much trauma to his strong body.

"The Military, the Army, that was his thing," said his son, Aaron. He was also a family man who put his family first and loved to be with them, to spend time with them and to make life an adventure for them. He was a hero to many, to his children, his wife and his cousins even before this tragedy struck.

He was the squad leader for the 1st Squadron, 14th Cavalry Regiment, of the Fort Lewis-based 3rd Brigade, 2nd Infantry

Division who is in Iraq. He is the 87th soldier from Ft. Lewis to be killed in Iraq since the U.S. invasion in March 2003.

At the service the Tacoma Police played the bagpipes, "Lament" and "Amazing Grace." I had heard the tunes played in Iraq more than once. It was played for soldiers who were killed and were ceremoniously escorted to an awaiting C-17. Their body was brought to the airfield in a Stryker vehicle, where their unit waited for them. The unit marched to the plane, formed a column through which the casket would pass and saluted as it did. There, these soldiers said farewell to a fallen comrade and were reminded of the reality of war and of the risk they lived daily, of their own vulnerability and of the cost of the service they were giving. Memories of watching this service filled my mind as I listened to the bagpipes in the main post chapel.

The minister told a story of a water carrier who daily filled two large pots, tied to a yolk he bore across his back. Each day he would go to the well and fill the pots and then carry them back to the village. One of the pots had a crack in it so that drops of water fell as he walked back along the path from the source of water to the village and when he arrived it would be only one half full. Such was the result of his labor, that only 1 ½ pots of water would be delivered. One day the pot with the defect spoke to the water carrier and apologized for not doing his job, for not bringing a full load to the village. The water carrier responded to the pot that he knew it had done its best and though it was not perfect, its crack had allowed drops of water to feed the land on that side of the path. There along the path were flowers growing which gladdened the heart and life of the water carrier. Along the side of the perfect pot, there were no flowers growing. In the cracked state the broken pot had given much to make the world a better place.

It was after Sgt. "K" was injured, cracked, that he continued to give and to share with his family and children his love and faith and strength which will forever stay in their hearts and make them better. His memory will never die and the strength of his last battle will build and support his family in their own trials of life.

It is also through our own weaknesses, the cracks in our lives, that we can and do build and strengthen others. Without knowing the pain and difficulty of life we could never lift and support others. There would be little compassion, little or no empathy, and thus I believe that we all have our cracks and we need to use those experiences to water the path, to feed the flowers and to make life better for others. If we were perfect with no flaws, or even put on the impression that we had no flaws, then no drops of living water would be released from our lives to help others. I recognize the flaws in my life and hopefully can strengthen others through them.

Sgt. 1st Class Kenneth Poturica talked of the hero that Henry had been and later called the "last roll." One name was called and a reply came back, "Here, Sergeant." A second, third and fourth names were called. A reply came back after each name, "Here, Sergeant." Then Sgt. Kalalewai was called. There was no response. "Sgt. Henry Kalalewai," the name rang out again and only silence could be heard. In earnest and with a pleading tone a third time, "Sgt. Henry K Kahalewai, Jr." was requested to reply, but there was quiet and hearts were filled with longing for an answer. After a pause the answer came, not a "Here, sir," but a reply from another voice, "He is not here, he has given his all, and will never answer roll call again, sir." A 21 gun salute sounded in 3 loud volleys at first jolting, startling in its volume and then the heart was stirred, being reminded of the blast which had injured and eventually taken his life.

In the end, the family was allowed to come forward and stand at his picture, at his boots, and remember him. The solders of his unit came forward, paused and saluted and moved silently on. A shell casing was left by many of these good men honoring Sgt. Kahalewai. I was able to join them in a salute to this good soldier and husband and father and then I went to tell his good wife and children that I was sorry, and that we loved and appreciated them.

The pain of the loss will linger, but so will the life of this good man. Debbie and her children will go to Hawaii for the final funeral and burial. They will come back and she will continue to work with us. I am thankful for that, for she is a good woman, a good nurse, a good person. I am thankful to the men and women who send their spouses to fight in this war, to the children who send their fathers and the parents who send their children, but there are no thanks which can take away the pain when one of them is lost.

The love will never die. Similar stories of strength and heroism could be shared and have been shared now about thousands of those valiant soldiers who have lost their lives in this war and in all wars for freedom from our past. I include only one here, but am thankful for each and every soldier who has given their life for our country and our world. Each has a story. May we remember them and never forget their sacrifice.

IN CONCLUSION

We are not fighting against Iraq, but against a large group of individuals whose goal it is to destroy any who do not side with them. They desire to spread their hate and power across that region and across the world.

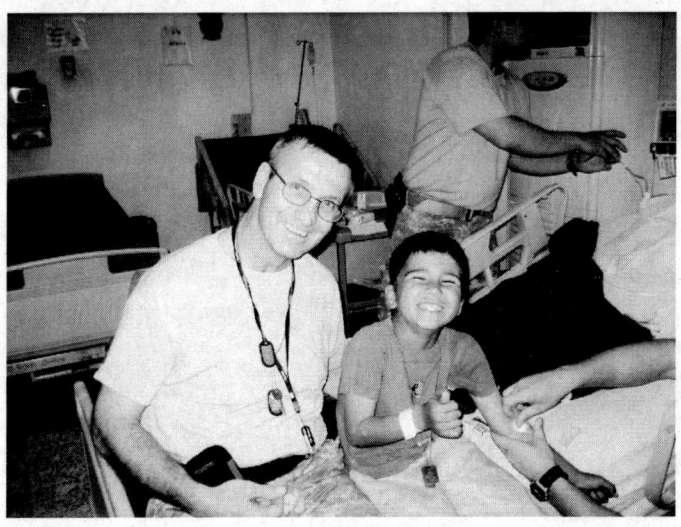

Dr. Faucette and one of the patients from the first Mass Casualty–Mosul, Iraq 2006.

To the soldier who has or will deploy, and to those who wonder about this war:

Since I have been back home I have had the opportunity to share my experiences with many groups. The most common question that I am asked is "Should we be in Iraq or not?" That is a difficult question and there is no simple answer. Congress, the President and the Military leaders are debating that from day to day. Second to that is the question, "Where do we go from here?"

Perhaps we should ask if we should have gone there in the first place. I believe that the decision to enter Iraq was an honest decision based upon the information that was available at the time. It was a very difficult decision and was not made without much thought. In retrospect, some of the data on which that decision was based has not proven to be true. Regardless of the reasons that we ended up in Iraq we find ourselves in a war and in the middle of a war between the groups of peoples in that country and region. We must move forward from where we are now.

I do not believe that war is a good thing. I do not believe that the loss of an American soldier is a good thing, and it is not easy to accept. I do not believe that hate, bombs and suppression are good things. How can we be victorious and not fight these things?

If we could magically solve things we would do it. If we could diplomatically work this out, get everyone concerned around a common table and come to a consensus which would result in freedom, security, peace and hope for all, we should do that. I really don't think that our enemies would be willing to sit down and talk as they do not have our same goals, objectives nor values.

The best answer I can recommend or think of is nation building. We have done that with some success, but we don't often hear those stories. We have many friends there, many who believe in the same things we believe in. The Koreans have helped build Iraq in the north with great success. If we could somehow help the Iraqi people build schools, educate their children, have meaningful jobs and meaningful lives, then we could make progress. If we could help them have a safe place to work and a safe place to sleep at night and celebrate in the day with good food, light and power, warmth in the winter and perhaps even air-conditioning in the hot summers, then we could make progress.

All of this is possible if the people could feel safe. They worry about their children being safe as they attend the bullet-riddled schools. Their streets are ever threatened by potential explosions which cause death and injury. If the people were safe, then the doctors and teachers would not leave the country. The scientists and engineers could build a better world for them. They have the oil, the fuel to make this happen. If we could help them farm and make the once fertile crescent again grow and produce, then they could help take care of themselves. There are two large rivers and flat land which once was fertile. Irrigation systems, fertilizer, sprinklers, tractors, combines and bailers could do a great job to make the country better.

To you who have fought there and have put your lives on the line for a cause, you should know that your effort has been for good. That cause which you have defended is to allow others the freedom that you and your children enjoy and to preserve that very freedom for your children and grandchildren. Future generations will face a much different world than you faced. No longer is war the blue versus the gray lining up and shooting at each other across a grassy field. No longer is war against an invading force which has marked planes, ships and tanks, with generals, captains, sergeants and privates in a different uniform. The enemy is not a country or the army of a country.

Today the enemy is an idea as well as all of those who are willing to kill because of that idea. The enemy is a cause which somehow is spread by watching someone else have "success" in random or directed explosions which kill and maim. Arms, legs and lives are taken. Children are as good a target as anyone else. If someone is willing to sacrifice their own child and themselves with explosives in a baby bottle or a diaper bag, as has been the case, then we have a challenge of knowing how to fight that enemy.

We are not fighting against Iraq, but against a large group of individuals whose goal it is to destroy any who do not side with them. They desire to spread their hate and power across that region and across the world. They desire to obtain lands and power which they feel were taken from them in the past, based on the belief that it ultimately is their destiny and that lands occupied in the past are divinely theirs forever. Such is the battle that you have fought or will fight. It will be the ride of your life for those who are still there or leaving.

For those who have returned home, you have learned a great deal. Your experience has been enlightening to you and to those with whom you have shared it. Life back home will be different. You will be different. Take what you have experienced and make your life and those of others better. Take more time to spend with your loved ones, to spend doing that which is important to you and your family. Be patient with yourself and with others. Talk to people if you are struggling. Your family also will need to be patient with you, will need to let you know that they missed you, but that they also grew and learned to survive with you gone. Be accepting of their growth and support them in it as well. Kids will have grown and changed. Catch up with them, love them and let them continue to grow. Time with your family is the most important time you can spend. Thanks for the sacrifice which you have given.

If America declares victory for what we have done as coalition forces and leave the country and region, the insurgents will say that they have really been the winners, for they are still there. "America has fled," they will say, and thus are cowards. Victory for the militants is to survive and still be able to spread their doctrines. They do not need to destroy our forces to have victory. Victory is not related to battles won or lost, to individual losses, but to survival and spread of their hate. If they survive, they can indoctrinate children. They can teach hate and intolerance. They can claim "Victory over America" as Saddam was wont to name one of his palaces. Perhaps they will be right.

I prefer "Victory with America," where their children are not facing explosions, injuries, loss of loved ones, friends and homes. I prefer that they could look forward with hope, with an ability to learn from books and from life. I prefer a place where they can seek God and have enough understanding to accept that others can believe differently and still be of worth as human beings.

The things I want for my children and family are the same things most people, most Iraqis, most Muslims want for theirs. It has been a privilege for me to have served in the cause.

I do not truly believe that we will ever be able to leave and declare a full victory, and I do not believe that we can stay as we are now. The militants, the insurgents, the terrorists, the bad men, the gangs, the evil will always be with us. The fight will always go on to some degree, and perhaps that is a fact we have to face, but not give in to.

As you try to answer the question of whether we should be there and where will we go in the coming weeks, months and years, I hope that you will consider some of the things I learned and shared in this enlightening experience. I hope that you will see not only the United States, but your vision will be expanded to the world and the small place in that world we call Iraq.

Thanks to you for choosing to read this book and considering those things. May the Lord bless you.

Sincerely,

COL Kelly J Faucette M.D.

Chief Department of Pediatrics

Madigan Army Medical Center

Staff physician, 47th CSH, Mosul, Iraq

CENTCOM Consultant for Pediatrics - Iraq

kandsfaucette@comcast.net

MILITARY TERMS—ACRONYMS

- CHU – Compartmentalized Housing Unit–our living quarters. They were non-permanent structures with lights, electricity and a window, but no water or other luxuries.
- CSH – Combat Support Hospital–a larger hospital of the military where patients are brought after being triaged and taken care of by medics or aid stations.
- FOB – The Forward Operating Base–a relatively secure area where central control of operations takes place.
- HUMVEE – previously known as a Hummer, a multipurpose vehicle akin to a large jeep.
- ICU – Intensive Care Unit–as in any hospital, where the most ill patients are cared for.
- IED – Improvised Explosive Devise–bombs made and hidden in anything and anywhere imaginable.
- LRMC – Landstuhl Regional Medical Center–A

medical center in Germany, a stop off place for many of the US patients returning to the states.

- MAMC – Madigan Army Medical Center–where I work in Tacoma, WA. Part of Ft. Lewis Army Base.
- MWR – Morale, Welfare and Recreation Center–A place where there are phones, TVs, computers, books, and other recreational needs, pool tables and the like.
- SPC – Specialist–an enlisted rank in the military between private and sergeant.
- VBIED – Vehicle Bourn Improvised Explosive Devise–a car bomb or a bomb placed in a truck.

ABOUT THE AUTHOR

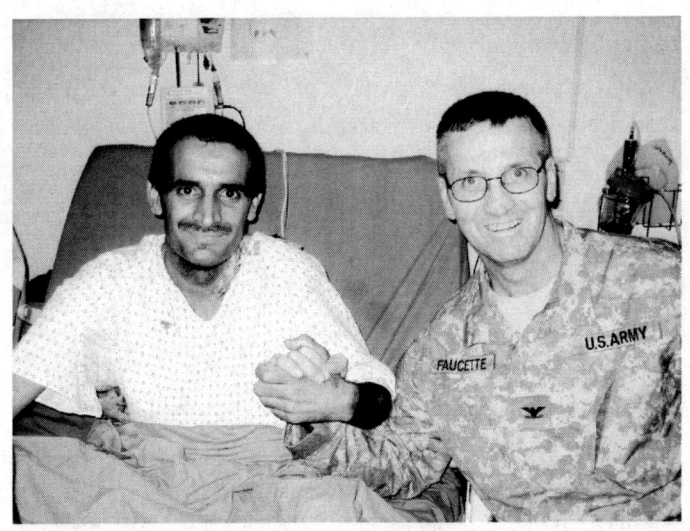

Dr. Faucette poses with one of his patients,
an Iraqi patient who was severely injured.

COL Kelly J Faucette is a pediatrician, a pediatric hematologist and oncologist. He specializes in the care of children with cancer, anemia and bleeding disorders. He found himself in somewhat unfamiliar territory at a combat support hospital, where the main problems were due to trauma, explosions, shrapnel and burns and also doing sick call for adults. Nevertheless over the years he had been well trained.

He grew up on a small farm in Colorado. He graduated from Sanford, CO High School with 18 other students and went to Adams State College in Alamosa, CO, for a year and then graduated from Brigham Young University. He went to medical school at the Uniformed Services University of Health Sciences, the military medical school in Bethesda, MD. Pediatric residency was at Fitzsimmons Army Medical Center in Aurora, CO, which since has closed. His formal education concluded after 27 years of school with a Hematology/Oncology fellowship at Primary Children's Hospital and the University of Utah in 1992. He has worn the army uniform for 28 years.

He is now a grandfather to a beautiful granddaughter and he and his wife, Sharon, have been married for 30 years. They have four children, two girls and two boys, Allyson, Kaylene, Garrett and Jordan. He has been the chief of pediatrics at Madigan Army Medical Center for over four years and had sent several physicians to Iraq to serve, so felt that it was his time to go and serve and thus in March 2006 he volunteered and left his family and friends for the ride of his life. While in Iraq he was awarded the bronze star for his work.

BIBLIOGRAPHY

1. CIA World Fact Book; Encyclopedia Britannica. The Middle East; A brief History of the Last 2000 Years, Bernard Lewis; TIME almanac.
2. Wikipedia–the free encyclopedia–on the internet